THE THEORY OF EDUCATION
IN THE UNITED STATES

by the same author

JEFFERSON

The Urquhart-le Motteux translation of
THE WORKS OF
FRANCIS RABELAIS
*Edited, with Introduction and Notes,
by Albert Jay Nock
and Catherine Rose Wilson*

THE THEORY OF EDUCATION
IN THE UNITED STATES

BY ALBERT JAY NOCK

THE PAGE-BARBOUR LECTURES FOR 1931
AT THE UNIVERSITY OF VIRGINIA

The Ludwig von Mises Institute
Auburn, Alabama
2007

Reprinted 2016 by the Luwig von Mises Institute.

Mises Institute
518 W Magnolia Ave
Auburn, AL 36832
mises.org

ISBN: 978-1-610160-94-0

PREFACE

THIS volume is made up of the Lectures delivered last year on the Page-Barbour Foundation, at the University of Virginia. They are threaded together to suit the requirements of publication, but are not much changed otherwise. The style of direct address is now regarded, I believe, as rather out of fashion for the printed page, but I have nevertheless decided, for the most part, to let it stand. I gratefully acknowledge the exquisite hospitality which the whole Academic Body of the University extended to these Lectures. Under the terms of the Foundation, they become, on delivery, the property of the University. Were they still mine, I should be much tempted to offer them as a tribute, *inane munus* indeed, but the best I have to offer, to the imperishable memory of that faithful and illustrious disciple of the Great Tradition, the University's Founder. Since they are quite unworthy of such a distinction, however, I am glad to be spared the pains of resisting that temptation.

ALBERT JAY NOCK.

THE THEORY OF EDUCATION
IN THE UNITED STATES

THE THEORY OF EDUCATION
IN THE UNITED STATES

I MAY be permitted to express my great pleasure in the welcome which you have accorded me. I am, of course, very happy to accept it as the official welcome extended to a servant who is borrowed for the occasion by one university from another. I trust, however, that you will allow me to regard it also as the impersonal welcome offered by citizens of the great republic of letters to another citizen whose only credentials and recommendations are those with which his citizenship provides him. I may moreover, I think, be permitted to assume that this impersonal hospitality will be extended to cover the consideration of the subject that I have been appointed to introduce. The constitution of our republic recognises no political boundaries, no distinctions of race or nation; our allegiance to it takes precedence over every local or personal interest. Our business here, I take it, is to consult about matters which seriously affect the welfare of our republic, and I may assume therefore that we are prepared to approach it in no provincial or parochial spirit, but in a truly republican frame of mind, intent only upon the interest to which our first allegiance is due, the interest of the republic of letters.

The subject that I am appointed to discuss is the theory of education in the United States. This discussion has its difficulties. It brings us face to face with a good many serious disappointments. It calls for the re-examination and criticism of a good many matters which seemed comfortably settled, and which we would rather leave undisturbed. The most discouraging difficulty about this discussion, however, is that apparently it cannot lead to any so-called practical conclusion; certainly not to any conclusion, as far as I can see, which will at all answer to the general faith in machinery as an effective substitute for thought, and the general reliance upon machinery alone to bring about any and all forms of social improvement. If Socrates had come before the Athenians with some fine new piece of machinery like a protective tariff, workmen's compensation, old-age pensions, collective ownership of the means of production, or what not; if he had told them that what they must do to be saved was simply to install his piece of machinery forthwith, and set it going; no doubt he would have interested a number of people, perhaps enough to put him in office as the standard-bearer of an enlightened and progressive liberalism. When he came before them, however, with nothing to say but *Know thyself*, they found his discourse unsatisfactory, and became impatient with him. So if a discussion of our educational theory could be made to lead to something that we might call "constructive"—that is to say, something that is immediately and mechanically practicable, like honour schools or a new type of housing or a new style of entrance examinations—one might hope to make it rather easily acceptable. There seems no way to do this. The only large reforms indicated by a thorough discussion of the topic are such as must be put down at once as quite impracticable on general grounds, and the minor mechanical changes that are indicated seem also impracticable on special grounds, besides having the appearance of uncertain value and therefore being unlikely to command interest. Yet notwithstanding this rather barren prospect for our discussion, one thing may perhaps redeem it from absolute sterility; which is that we are presumably always better off for knowing just where we are, and for being able to identify and measure the forces which are at play upon us. I do not wish to adduce too depressing a parallel in saying that diagnosis has value even in a hopeless case. Hopelessness in many cases, for instance in cases of incipient tuberculosis, as you know, is circumstantial, and circumstances may change; it is almost never flatly impossible that they should change. Diagnosis, then, has obvious value when it shows only that *in those circumstances* the case is hopeless; and even when it reveals the case as hopeless in any circumstances, it affords at least the melancholy satisfaction of knowing just where one stands.

We may observe then, in the first place, that our educational system has always been the object of strong adverse criticism. No one has ever been especially well satisfied with it, or well pleased with the way it worked; no one, I mean, whose opinion was at the same time informed and disinterested, and therefore worth attention. Late in the last century, Ernest Renan said that "countries which, like the United States, have set up a considerable popular instruction without any serious higher education, will long have to expiate their error by their intellectual mediocrity, the vulgarity of their manners, their superficial spirit, their failure in general intelligence." This is very hard language, and I do not propose, for the moment, that we should undertake to say how far its severity may be fairly regarded as justifiable. I may, however, ask you to notice two things; first, the distinction which M. Renan draws between instruction and education, and second, his use of the word *intelligence*. We shall not lay down a definition of education in set terms here at the outset of our discussion; I think it would be more satisfactory if, with your permission, we should gradually work towards the expression of our idea of what education is, and of what an educated person is like. It is sometimes, indeed often, difficult to construct in set terms the definition of an object which we nevertheless recognise at once for what it is, and about which we have no possible manner of doubt. I could not to save my life, for instance, make a definition of an oyster; yet I am sure I know an oyster when I see one. Moreover, in looking at an oyster, I can point out a number of differentiations, more or less rough and superficial, perhaps, but quite valid in helping to determine my knowledge. So in gradually building up an expression of our idea of education, we find the distinction drawn by M. Renan especially useful. Perhaps we are not fully aware of the extent to which instruction and education are accepted as being essentially the same thing. I think you would find, if you looked into it, for instance, that all the formal qualifications for a teacher's position rest on this understanding. A candidate is certificated—is he not?—merely as having been exposed satisfactorily to a certain kind of instruction for a certain length of time, and therefore he is assumed eligible to a position which we all agree that only an educated person should fill. Yet he may not be at all an educated person, but only an instructed person. We have seen many such, and five minutes' talk with one of them is quite enough to show that the understanding of instruction as synonymous with education is erroneous. They are by no means the same thing. Let us go no further at present in trying to determine what education is, but merely take note that it is not the same thing as instruction. Let us keep that differentiation in mind, never losing sight of it for a moment, and considering carefully every point in the practice of pedagogy at which it is applicable. If we do this, I venture to predict that we shall turn up an astonishing number of such points, and that our views of current pedagogy will be very considerably modified in consequence. An educated man must be in some sort instructed; but it is a mere *non distributio medii* to say that an instructed person must be an educated person.

An equally useful distinction comes out in M. Renan's use of the word *intelligence*. To most of us, I think, that word does not mean the same thing that it means to a Frenchman, or that the word *Intelligenz* means to a German. To a Frenchman like M. Renan, intelligence does not mean a quickness of wit, a ready dexterity in handling ideas, or even a ready accessibility to ideas. It implies those, of course, but it does not mean them; and one should perhaps say in passing that it does not mean the pert and ignorant cleverness that current vulgar usage has associated with the word. Again it is our common day-to-day experience that gives us the best possible assistance in establishing the necessary differentiations. We have all seen men who were quick-witted, accessible to ideas and handy with their management of them, whom we should yet hesitate to call intelligent; we are conscious that the term does not quite fit. The word sends us back to a phrase of Plato. The person of intelligence is the one who always tends to "see things as they are," the one who never permits his view of them to be directed by convention, by the hope of advantage, or by an irrational and arbitrary authoritarianism. He allows the current of his consciousness to flow in perfect freedom over any object that may be presented to it, uncontrolled by prejudice, prepossession or formula; and thus we may say that there are certain integrities at the root of intelligence which give it somewhat the aspect of a moral as well as an intellectual attribute.

Besides having laid up the benefit of a couple of extremely valuable fundamental distinctions, we are now perhaps in a position to discern more clearly the force of M. Renan's criticism of our educational system. Some ten or fifteen years after M. Renan made these observations, we find a curious corroboration of them which is especially worth citing because it was made by one upon whom no suspicion of superciliousness can rest. Walt Whitman was "the good grey poet" of the common life, the prophet of the social mean. His love for America and his faith in its institutions may, I believe, be admitted without question. His optimism was robust and obtrusive; one might call it flagrant. Yet we find him reflecting with great severity upon "a certain highly deceptive superficial popular intellectuality" which he found existing in our society of the late 'seventies. He goes beyond this to say that "our New World Democracy," whatever its success in other directions, "is, so far, an almost complete failure in its social aspects, and in really grand religious, moral, literary and æsthetic results." M. Renan was a foreigner and an academician, and his criticism, we may say, is to be taken subject to discount; he could not be expected to appraise properly the spirit of America. Well, but, here we have Whitman who was just the opposite of a foreigner and an academician, who is accepted everywhere and by all as of the very spirit of America—here we have Whitman bearing out M. Renan's criticism at every point. What is an educational system for, one may ask, if not to produce social results precisely opposite to those which M. Renan testified before the fact, and Whitman testified after the fact, were characteristic of our country? If our system, then, could do no better than it was doing, it should be forthwith taken in hand and overhauled.

II

Taken in hand it accordingly was, about thirty-five years ago, and very energetically. Dissatisfaction focussed about the thesis that our system was out of relation to life. Something must be done with it to make our children grow up as men of their time, and prepare them to face actuality. Too much attention had been paid to the languages, literature and history of classical antiquity, which were all of far less than doubtful value to the youth of twentieth-century America. The thing now was to introduce the sciences, living languages and the useful arts, to make instruction vocational, to open all manner of opportunities for vocational study, and to induce youth into our institutions for pretty strictly vocational purposes. All this was done; the process amounted to a revolution, carried out with extraordinary thoroughness and in an astonishingly short time. Hardly any débris of the old order remains except, curiously, the insignia of certain proficiencies; these now survive as mere vestiges. You are as well aware as I, for example, of what a bachelor's degree in the liberal arts now represents. Some new insignia have been devised, and one or two borrowed from the systems of other countries, like the degree of doctor of philosophy, which fulfils the humble but possibly necessary function of a factory-inspection label, some say a trade-union label; perhaps it is both. Aside from these insignia, however, nothing is left; our system underwent a revolutionary renovation. Exponents of the new order have had their way unhindered, and have been able to command an almost inconceivable amount of money and enthusiasm in support of their plans and policies.

Yet after three decades of this, our system gives no better satisfaction, apparently, than it did before. At no time during this period has it given satisfaction; hence the period has been one of incessant tinkering, the like of which probably has never been seen anywhere in the world. Method after method, device after device, readjustment after readjustment, have been tried, scrapped, revived and modified, and then tried again. One might say that the field of our pedagogy during these three decades has been the drillground of empiricism; large areas of it, indeed, seem to have been, and still seem to be, the hunting-ground of quackery. One cannot too much wonder at the high hopefulness attending this unconscionable revel of experimentation. Yes, yes, we kept saying, let us but just install this one new method in the secondary schools, or this one new set of curricular changes in the undergraduate college, or this one grand new scheme for broadening the scope of university instruction, and in a year or so it will prove itself to be the very thing we have all along been needing; and this, that or the other batch of pedagogical problems will be laid to eternal rest. Such, I think, is a fair summary of our thirty years' experience; the details of it are no doubt well known to you, and many of them will probably recur to your memory at once, perhaps in some cases with a rather strong appeal to your sense of humour.

Ingenuity, however, when applied *in limine*,

must some time reach the end of its exercise, and that time seems now to have come. We seem now to be at the moment when every conceivable mode of tinkering has been applied at every available point in our educational system, and when nobody can think of anything more to do. Professional educators are carrying on as best they can, occasionally pausing to consider the gains which accrued from the revolution of thirty years ago, and which the efforts of three decades have been devoted to consolidating. From what some of them say, it might appear that these gains are relatively inconsiderable, hardly worth the crushing price set by the turmoil of a revolution and the distracting toil of consolidation. Many professional educators, even some veterans of the revolution who fought behind the barricades and manfully worked the guillotine in the hour of triumph—even some of these seem now to be in the mood of self-examination, wondering, like Mr. Weller's charity-boy at the end of the alphabet, whether it was worth going through so much to get so little. Dissatisfaction is, of course, a noble and invaluable attribute of man; one should never, strictly speaking, be satisfied with anything, least of all with the social institutions and mechanisms which we create. The lively and peremptory exercise of dissatisfaction is the first condition of progress; one wishes that Americans at large had a better understanding of its uses. But dissatisfaction with something which may and should be made to work better, differs in quality from dissatisfaction with something which gives no hope of ever being made to work at all. Dissatisfaction in the realm of the aëroplane is a very different thing in quality from dissatisfaction in the realm of the perpetual-motion device. In the one case, the application of ingenuity may, and often does, improve the machine and makes it work better. In the other case, when all the resources of ingenuity are exhausted, the machine gives only a semblance of working, without the reality.

In criticism of the present state of our educational system, non-professional opinion appears to be in pretty close agreement with the opinion lately expressed by many of our professional educators.

THE THEORY OF EDUCATION

A few months ago, an Italian nobleman, one of
the most accomplished men in Europe, told me
that he had had a curious experience in our country; he wondered whether I had made anything
like the same observation, and if so, how I accounted for it. He said he had been in America
several times, and had met some very well-educated men, as an Italian would understand the
term; but they were all in the neighbourhood of
sixty years old. Under that age, he said, he had
happened upon no one who impressed him as at
all well-educated. I told him that he had been
observing the remnant of a pre-revolutionary
product, and coming from a country that had had
the Sicilian Vespers and Rienzi and Massaniello
and now Mussolini, he should easily understand
what that meant; that our educational system had
been thoroughly reorganised, both in spirit and
structure, about thirty-five years ago, and that his
well-educated men of sixty or so were merely
holdovers from what we now put down, by general consent, as the times of ignorance—holdovers
from pre-Fascist days, if I might borrow the com-

parison. "But," I went on, "our younger men are really very keen; they are men of parts, and our schools and universities do an immense deal for them. Just try to come round one of them about the merits of a bond-issue or a motor-car, the fine points of commercial cake-icing or retail shoe-merchandising, or the problems of waste motion involved in bricklaying or in washing dishes for a hotel, and you are sure to find that he will give a first-rate account of himself, and that he reflects credit on the educational system that turned him out." My friend looked at me a moment in a vacant kind of way, and presently said that proficiency in these pursuits was not precisely what he had in mind when he spoke of education. "Just so," I replied, "but it is very much what we have in mind. We are all for being practical in education. Do you know, it would not surprise me in the least to find that our Russian friends had taken a leaf out of our book in designing their Five-Year Plan?" He looked at me again for a moment, and changed the subject. I thought of explaining myself, but saw it would be of no use; my little pleas-

THE THEORY OF EDUCATION

antry had been dashed to pieces against the solid adamant of his patrician seriousness.

It is unquestionably an interesting problem that is set for us by the fact that with everything its own way, with no lack of means or moral support, our system should bring forth secondary schools which lie helpless under the formidable indictment of Mr. Learned, and universities which lie helpless under the equally formidable indictment of Mr. Flexner. As for our undergraduate colleges, the president of Columbia University, Mr. Butler, was quoted in the press only the other day as saying that they had been trying all through the post-revolutionary period to find an effective substitute for their discarded curriculum, and had not yet succeeded.* I may remind you of similarly depressing utterances made recently by the late president of Brown, the president of Haverford, Mr. Gauss of Princeton, the late Mr. Giddings of Columbia, and many others. An inquiry made last

* The last annual report of the Carnegie Foundation, published while this volume was in the press, contains most astonishing testimony on this point.

winter into New York City's elementary schooling reached the conclusion that many more than one-third of the pupils cannot be dragged through the work assigned them; and this in spite of considerable official pressure upon teachers to promote pupils without too close regard to the quality of their work. At the fifty-fifth anniversary of the founding of Johns Hopkins University, Mr. Lang said that the type of education offered in our new million-dollar high schools is about one-twentieth as valuable as the kind given in the traditional little red schoolhouse of a generation ago. Last spring, at a conference of educators in Florida, there was practical unanimity, according to the press reports, in the opinion that our educational system is a failure. Mr. Butler again, in a public utterance, permits himself the desponding observation that the results of our educational endeavours "are admitted to be anything but satisfactory." Only the other day, the head master of Harrow, speaking of the corruption that has set in upon our English speech, observed that England is "exposed to the whole backwash of the

United States, where there are a hundred million people who have very little literary tradition."

I need not continue these depressing citations; you may carry them to any length you like by following the newspapers from week to week. There seems no room for doubt that the quality of our educational system's product is as unfavourably regarded now as it was thirty-five years ago, and that the force of criticism, professional and lay, against our system has not abated, but rather the contrary. While the systems of Holland, Scandinavia, Belgium, Germany, France, with little money and relatively poor equipment, keep turning out at least a moderately acceptable product, our rich and well-equipped foundations elaborate a product that is on all sides regarded as quite unacceptable. This is a strange state of things, and as I have said, it presents an interesting problem for our examination; a problem which we may presently consider.

III

I HAVE mentioned the fact that our system has been subjected to incessant tinkering throughout the post-revolutionary period. We may now observe that all this tinkering has been purely mechanical and external; it has been applied exclusively to the structure and mechanics of the system. We have devised or imported the mechanics of this or that method, and sought to incorporate them; the inductive method, the Gary method, the Montessori method, and so on. We have scrapped one piece of curricular machinery after another, and introduced new ones. I do not recall the names of more than one or two of them, they are so many and have come and gone in such quick succession. Lately, however, as I remember, we have been hearing about the University of Wisconsin plan, the University of Chicago plan, the Harvard plan, and I think I recall seeing somewhere that Yale has recently come forward with a new plan, abolishing certain courses and certain examinations, and introducing something called "reading periods" by way of substitute. I do not speak in disparagement of these innumerable plans and methods, for I do not know enough about them to criticise them either favourably or unfavourably. I am a man of letters, not a mechanician or an actuary, and hence my opinion of their specific merit or lack of merit is without value. I merely ask you to remark that they are of a purely mechanical nature, and that as far as I know, all the effort that has been expended on improving our system during the last thirty-five years has been directed exclusively towards its mechanics.

Now, we may admit that our system, like any other social institution, is a machine, and that any machine is all the better for very careful tending, and that most machines are susceptible of further differentiation and improvement. Whatever care and ingenuity, therefore, has been exercised in these directions in behalf of our educational system has perhaps been well spent. But there is something more to be thought of. Any machine has some kind of theory behind it; and when you have

IN THE UNITED STATES

a machine that has had every possible resource of mechanical ingenuity and care expended on it, and yet will not work satisfactorily, the situation at once suggests that something may be amiss with its theory. Perhaps its theory is all wrong, hopelessly wrong; the perpetual-motion devices that we occasionally hear of are instances of this. They are, let us say, mechanically perfect, and as far as mechanics go, they should work perfectly, but they do not work; so we examine their theory, and we at once discover not only why they do not work but also why no machine of the kind can possibly work. Again, perhaps there has been some little slip somewhere in our apprehension of the theory, something overlooked, some minor error that needs to be straightened out, and the structure of our machine correspondingly modified. Well, this can be managed, possibly with ease, possibly the necessary adjustments are slight and simple; but the theory of the machine must be re-examined before anything can be done intelligently. My point is that a complete and clear idea of the theory behind a machine, is valuable; and that as far as I am aware, with all the attention that has been bestowed on the mechanics of our educational system, no one has looked critically into its theory. Perhaps the time for that has only now come. At all events, since we have quite reached the end of our tether in the mechanics of the matter—there seems to be no possible doubt of that—and since we are mostly, save for the Micawbers and Panglosses among us, looking at one another in a rather bewildered and forlorn way, wondering what to do next, we may at least passively entertain the idea of examining the theory of the thing with which we have been so long hopefully tinkering.

IV

FIRST, then, we may remark that at the root of that theory (not, indeed, forming a part of it, but of great influence in shaping it and getting it translated into practice) lay one of the most humane, honourable and engaging sentiments that are in the power of human nature to generate or to indulge. I refer to the sentiment which prompted our ancestors to determine that their children should have a better chance at the good life, the humane life, than circumstances had permitted themselves to have. If you go through our literature with an eye out for evidences of this sentiment, I think you may be astonished to see how constantly they appear, and I am sure you will be touched by their profound and pathetic eloquence. I am sure, too, that you will be interested in observing the number of points in our institutional life that this sentiment has touched, and in marking the reach of its power. I greatly doubt that a similar sentiment has ever held so commanding a position in the development of any modern society. It would be an easy and pleasant task to dwell on instances of that sentiment's operation, to remark the uncomplaining acquiescence in great personal sacrifices which its indulgence involved. But this is not necessary; we have all seen such instances, no doubt some of us have participated in them as beneficiaries. We have said enough, I think, to show with what veneration we should regard this sentiment, and with what delicacy we should speak of it even when we are obliged to regard its exercise as misdirected; for seriously misdirected it often was, and often is. We may observe, we must in justice observe, that this sentiment has often been very imperfectly and poorly interpreted by those who indulged it most prodigally; and never oftener than now. Its interpretation frequently betrays a vast ignorance of what the humane life really is, and of the discipline whereby alone one may make progress towards this life. We must judge these misinterpretations impartially and severely, for if they are not so judged before the tribunal of letters, they will be judged nowhere else; there is no other court competent to pass judgment on them. But our very impartiality and our commitment to severity are such as powerfully reinforce our natural disposition to maintain a just reverence for the nobleness and purity of the sentiment itself.

This sentiment, I say, served as a quickening spirit, not an enlightening spirit. Its ministrations moved us to the construction, by no means deliberate but quite at haphazard, of an educational theory which may be decomposed into three basic ideas or principles. The first idea was that of equality; the second, that of democracy; and the third idea was that the one great assurance of good public order and honest government lay in a literate citizenry. I need not remind you of Mr. Jefferson's passionate faith in this third idea, and his insistence upon it in season and out of season. It was in his day a speculative idea, which commanded quite wide consent among thoughtful persons, but which the subsequent test of practice has rather tended to explode. These three ideas are the fundamental ones in our theory of education today, precisely as they were in Mr. Jefferson's time. They remain unmodified, and even, as I said, unexamined; they are taken as axiomatic, and all the mechanism of our system, the whole of our pedagogical practice from the primary school to the university, is built upon them.

These ideas or principles, then, are what we must consider if we propose to turn from the mechanics of our system to its theory. If we find anything wrong with them, anything unsound, we may at once apply our findings to see how the working of our mechanism is affected, and what results a clarification or straightening-up of our theory in those respects might be presumed to have.

Let us proceed, then, to examine the first of these principles, the principle of equality. We need bring forward no evidence that the doctrine of equality is a sound one, or to prove that Menander was as right in his exhortation to "choose equality" as he was in his observation that "evil communications corrupt good manners." The idea of equality was very much abroad in the land in the early days of the republic; the French revolutionary formula of "liberty, equality, fraternity" helped in keeping it to the fore. But we perceive at once the necessity of discriminating between a sound philosophical doctrine, such as the doctrine of equality is, and the popular formulation of that doctrine, which may be fantastically unsound. There is usually a great difference between these two, as great a difference, as a rule, as there is between truth and untruth. The classical example, probably, is that of Christian doctrine. Again, the doctrine of Socialism, or of Communism, is one thing, and the set of fanciful credenda which popular imagination has conceived of as belonging to it is quite another thing; for instance, the curious notion which you find widely held, that Socialism has for its aim the arbitrary division of the world's wealth among its population, men, women and children, share and share alike. Again, the doctrine of the single tax is almost universally believed to concern a tax on land, which is precisely what it does not at all concern, instead of a hundred-per-cent tax on the rent of land. Thus, again, the doctrine of equality and its corollaries and implications have undergone the most astounding popular misunderstanding; you may remember, perhaps, the humorous and not much exaggerated popular formulation of it in the saying that "in the United States one man is just exactly as good as another, or a little better." Indeed, in the social sphere, the doctrine of equality has regularly been degraded into a kind of charter for rabid self-assertion on the part of ignorance and vulgarity; in the political sphere it has served as a warrant for the most audacious and flagitious exercise of self-interest. So, when we set about the examination of this doctrine in relation to our educational system, we must first and above all ascertain which doctrine of equality it is that we find at the basis of our system; is it the philosophical doctrine recommended by Menander and espoused by Mr. Jefferson, or is it a popular doctrine which neither of them could or would recognise?

There is no possible doubt about the answer. Our system is based upon the assumption, popularly regarded as implicit in the doctrine of equality, that everybody is educable. This has been taken without question from the beginning; it is taken without question now. The whole structure of our system, the entire arrangement of its mechanics, testifies to this. Even our truant laws testify to it, for they are constructed with exclusive reference to school-age, not to school-ability. When we attempt to run this assumption back to the philosophical doctrine of equality, we cannot do it; it is not there, nothing like it is there. The philosophical doctrine of equality gives no more ground for the assumption that all men are educable than it does for the assumption that all men are six feet tall. We see at once, then, that it is not the philosophical doctrine of equality, but an utterly untenable popular perversion of it, that we find at the basis of our educational system.

We shall probably recur to this doctrine later by a round-about way. For the present we may dismiss our *a priori* consideration of it with a single interesting and significant reference. We may believe, I think, that no more sincere believer in the doctrine of equality ever lived than Mr. Jefferson;

certainly none more intelligent; yet the plan that he drafted for public education in the State of Virginia is the severest possible judgment against the popular perversion which we have followed ever since his day, and are still following. Mr. Chinard, of the Faculty of Literature at Johns Hopkins, who probably knows more about Mr. Jefferson than any one else in the country knows, thinks that his plan may have had a good deal to do with shaping the French system, which, as you know, differs from ours in being rigidly selective. In outline, Mr. Jefferson's plan was this: Every child in the State should be taught reading, writing and common arithmetic; the old-fashioned primary-school course in the three Rs. Each year the best pupil in each primary school should be sent to the grammar schools, of which there were to be twenty, conveniently located in various parts of the State; they were to be kept there one or two years, and then dismissed, except "the best genius of the whole," who should be continued there for the full term of six years. "By this means," wrote Mr. Jefferson, "twenty of the best geniuses shall be raked from the rubbish annually." I venture to call your attention to these rather forceful words, as showing how far this great believer in equality was from anything like acceptance of our official assumption that everybody is educable. But this is not all. At the end of six years the best ten out of the twenty should be sent to William and Mary College, and the rest turned adrift. Mr. Jefferson's plan appears selective with a vengeance in our eyes, accustomed as they are to the spectacle of immense hordes of inert and ineducable persons slipping effortlessly through our secondary schools, colleges, universities, on ways that seem greased for their especial benefit. Of the twenty best geniuses annually raked from the rubbish of a whole State, only fifty per cent were destined to reach the undergraduate college!

The second idea which we are to examine is that of democracy; our system is professedly democratic. Let us see what this means. Here we find something more than a popular perversion of a philosophically sound doctrine, which is what we found in our examination of the idea of equality.

THE THEORY OF EDUCATION

Here we find something even stranger and more interesting, a perversion upon a perversion. Political theory of the eighteenth century was based upon the right of individual self-expression in politics; its essence was that those who vote, rule. Its chosen machinery was that of a republic, as affording the best power or purchase for the free expression of this right. As a matter of logic, when everybody votes, you have a democracy; the registration of democratic judgment is a mere matter of counting ballots. Thus a confusion of terms set in; a republic in which everybody voted was accepted as a democracy and was so styled, as it still is. This confusion persists, and the evidence of it is on every other page of many, I think the great majority, of serious writers. In fact, we may say that the terms *republican* and *democratic* have come to be regarded as synonymous. This is not greatly to be wondered at, because it is only lately that anything like a general sense of the unsoundness of eighteenth-century political theory has begun to prevail. The iron force of circumstance has finally made us aware that it is not, never was and never will be, those who vote that rule, but those who own; that you may extend the suffrage in a republic as far as you please without making any significant change in the actual rulership of the country. Republicanism does not, therefore, of itself even imply democracy. At the present time it is a matter of open and notorious knowledge that some monarchies are much more forward in democracy than some republics, even republics in which suffrage is universal. The antithesis of republicanism is monarchy, if you like, but monarchy is not the antithesis of democracy. The antithesis of democracy is absolutism; and absolutism may, and notoriously does, prevail under a republican régime as freely as under any other. Thus democracy is not a matter of an extension of the franchise, not a matter of the individual citizen's right of self-expression in politics, as the political philosophy of the eighteenth century regarded it. It is a matter of the diffusion of ownership; a true doctrine of democracy is a doctrine of public property.

A philosophical historian measures the value of

a revolution, not by its political achievements, not by the various social emancipations and ameliorations that it brings about, but by the quality of the idea that it liberates upon the world. The idea of the right of individual self-expression in politics had been formulated before 1789, it had been advanced and advocated by social philosophers, but the French Revolution liberated it, diffused it everywhere, made its terms a common glossary. Just so the Russian Revolution liberated the idea that democracy is not a political status at all, but an economic status. This idea also had long been accepted by many social philosophers. It was implicit in the doctrine of the Physiocrats, of Gumplovicz of Graz, of Theodor Hertzka, explicitly recognised by Marx, and elaborated in our own country by Henry George. But the explosion of the Russian Revolution liberated the idea, blew it, we may say, into all men's heads and lodged it fast there, so that now, consciously or unconsciously, intelligently or unintelligently, they interpret democracy to themselves in some kind of economic terms. This revelation of democracy as an economic status was no doubt purely a byeproduct of the Russian Revolution; such, too, was the idea liberated by the French Revolution. Revolutionists do not habitually think in academic terms. But it is by the quality of the liberated idea, not by the ups and downs of the Five-Year Plan, not by the ups and downs of organised Communism, not by the merits or demerits of any social or administrative machinery peculiar to the Soviet régime, that the philosophical historian will estimate the real significance of the Russian Revolution.

We see, then, that the political philosophy of the eighteenth century had a wholly erroneous notion of the nature of democracy, and that it was this erroneous notion which has lasted all through our history, namely: that democracy is a political status, and that it is to be achieved or realised by an extension of the franchise. Meanwhile, on the top of this, which we may call an academic error, grew the popular error which accepted as democratic whatever was merely indiscriminate. This error, too, has persisted down to our time. The people of Philadelphia in Genêt's day, who wore cockades in their hats and called one another "citizen" no doubt believed that they were giving an exhibition of democratic manners. They were not; they were giving an exhibition of bizarre manners, vulgar manners. It is a commonplace of our journalism to speak of some highly-placed person as having democratic manners when he is only affable, or sometimes when he is only coarse and rude. There is no such thing as democratic manners; manners are either bad or good. "A man thinks to show himself my equal by showing himself *grob*," said Heine; "he does not show himself my equal; he shows himself *grob*."

Interested popular definition, like interested legal definition, is a process, as a contemporary of Bishop Butler said, by which anything can be made to mean anything. The popular idea of democracy is animated by a very strong resentment of superiority. It resents the thought of an élite; the thought that there are practicable ranges of intellectual and spiritual experience, achievement and enjoyment, which by nature are open to some and not to all. It deprecates and disallows this thought, and discourages it by every available means. As the popular idea of equality postulates that in the realm of the spirit everybody is able to enjoy everything that anybody can enjoy, so the popular idea of democracy postulates that there shall be nothing worth enjoying for anybody to enjoy that everybody may not enjoy; and a contrary view is at once exposed to all the evils of a dogged, unintelligent, invincibly suspicious resentment.

The whole institutional life organised under the popular idea of democracy, then, must reflect this resentment. It must aim at no ideals above those of the average man; that is to say, it must regulate itself by the lowest common denominator of intelligence, taste and character in the society which it represents. In a society governed by this idea, for example, schools like the Crown Patronage Schools of Prussia would be resented as undemocratic. The advantage of such schools, obviously, is, first, that of being founded by a sovereign whose position raises him above a great many petty and local considerations, and thus largely enables him to view their plan disinterestedly; and second, that the sovereign can command not only the most competent but also the most disinterested advice. Hence they would probably be better schools than those which might be set up by a local school-board appointed by a mayor or elected by popular vote. The spirit of democracy, however, would look askance at schools established by an absolute sovereign, with the advice of men like von Humboldt and Schleiermacher, because in its view the first business of a school is not to be good, but as our phrase goes, "to give the people what they want"; and this is what the school set up by the mayor and school-board is much more likely to do. Animating this view is the touchy and resentful assurance that it is no sovereign's or scholar's business to suggest what the people should want or might profitably want; who is any von Humboldt or Schleiermacher that he should offer gratuitous advice about what our children should learn or how they should be taught?

We perceive at once, of course, that all this has actually nothing to do with democracy; but quite clearly it is all in the popular interpretation of democracy, and it is with this, rather than with any rational notion of democracy, that our educational system has always been obliged to reckon. We must face the fact, and we may face it with the dignity and disinterestedness appropriate to scholars, that an examination of our system from end to end shows its theory to be as unsound in respect to democracy as we found it to be in respect of equality. Look at it anywhere, strike into it at any point you like, and the working of its mechanism will testify to a theory that is not equalitarian but pseudo-equalitarian; a theory that is not democratic, but egregiously and preposterously pseudo-democratic.

V

WITH regard to the third idea that enters into our educational theory, the idea that good government and a generally wholesome public order are conditioned upon having a literate citizenry, not much need be said. We have already mentioned Mr. Jefferson's strong insistence on this doctrine, and we may now recall the warmth and enthusiasm that he showed for it in a letter congratulating a Spanish correspondent on some steps that the Spanish Government was proposing to take against illiteracy. Mr. Jefferson's reasoning was that citizens who could read had the means of being correctly informed about public affairs, and that if they were correctly informed they might be trusted to do the right thing about them. There are certain defects in this reasoning upon which we need not dwell. We may observe, however, without at all disparaging literacy, that in general the mere ability to read raises no very extravagant presumptions upon the person who has it. Surely everything depends upon what he reads, and upon the purpose that guides him in reading it. It is interesting to note that one who might be called Mr. Jefferson's contemporary (he died when Mr. Jefferson was nine years old) furnishes us with precisely the right criticism upon this point. This was Joseph Butler, bishop of Durham, the revered author of the *Analogy*, and one of the four greatest in all the Church of England's long roster of great men. Bishop Butler made the acute observation that the majority of men are much more apt at passing things through their minds than they are at thinking about them. Hence, he said, considering the kind of thing we read and the kind of attention we bestow on it, very little of our time is more idly spent than the time spent in reading. For evidence of this one has but to look at our large literate population, to remark its intellectual interests, the general furniture of its mind, as these are revealed by what it reads; by the colossal, the unconscionable, volume of garbage annually shot upon the public from the presses of the country, largely in the form of newspapers and periodicals.

On the other hand, too, we may regard the negative testimony furnished by the extremely exiguous existence among us of anything like a serious literature, especially a serious periodical literature. It must be clear, I think, that any expectations put upon the saving grace of literacy are illusory.

We have found, then, three most serious errors in the theory upon which the mechanics of our educational system were designed. This theory contemplates a fantastic and impracticable idea of equality, a fantastic and impracticable idea of democracy, and a fantastically exaggerated idea of the importance of literacy in assuring the support of a sound and enlightened public order. It is not necessary, I think, to go further in the examination of our educational theory, after finding in it three errors of the first magnitude. We may now go on to observe how directly certain structural defects and mechanical failures in our system, and certain misconceptions of function as well, are traceable to these errors of theory. Before doing so, however, let us notice how well these errors complement one another, and how orderly they fall in behind the admirable sentiment that we noticed at the outset of our discussion. First, there was this strong sentiment for one's children, and for their progress in a civilised life. The conception of a civilised life, of its nature, and of the way to enter into it, was and is often most imperfect, but no matter; the sentiment was in itself noble and disinterested. One's children should have, at any cost or sacrifice, all the education they could get. Then, playing directly into the hand of this sentiment, there was the idea of equality prompting the belief that they were all capable of taking in and assimilating what there was to be had; and then the idea of democracy, prompting the belief that the whole subject-matter of education should be common property, not common in a true and proper sense, but, roughly, in the sense that so much of it as was not manageable by everybody should be disallowed and disregarded. Then finally, all this had the general sanction of a pseudo-patriotic idea that in thus doing one's best for one's children, one was also doing something significant in the way of service to one's country.

You may see easily, I think, how this theory would work out in practice, and what sort of mechanism would naturally be required to make it effective; hence you may see just what sort of educational system would grow up under the conditions set by this theory. I think further that if you compare the kind of system that you thus imagine with the system that we actually have, you will find a very close correspondence between them; and that the more you particularise the comparison, point by point, the closer you will find the correspondence to be.

VI

TRADITIONALLY, an educational system was conceived of as an organic whole, with distinct lines fixed between its units; and each unit was supposed to exercise its function with strict reference to the units preceding and succeeding it. When we organised our system, this was also our general plan. Our units were the primary and secondary schools, the undergraduate college, the university and the technical school. The intention was that a person should proceed directly through the primary school into the secondary school, and through that into the undergraduate college. On leaving college, he was prepared to enter the university, if he was looking forward to one of the four so-called "learned" professions. Otherwise, if he proposed to occupy himself with one of the sciences, or with some pursuit like agriculture, architecture, engineering, for which a considerable technical training is necessary, he was also prepared

THE THEORY OF EDUCATION

to begin that; he was qualified to enter the institute of science or the technical school. I do not say that this intention was always and everywhere carried out; at the University of Paris, in the sixteenth century, students entered under the Faculty of Law with very little preparation, sometimes with none. In a new civilisation like ours, local poverty, poor equipment, the scarcity of teachers, and other difficult obstacles stood in the way of orderly consecutive progress through all these grades. Nevertheless, this was the intention; and in general, probably, it was as well kept to as circumstances permitted.

The intention was, moreover—and this is most important—that the character of this progress through the schools and the undergraduate college, right up to the doors of the university or technical school, should be purely disciplinary. The curricula of the primary and secondary school and of the college should be fixed, invariable, the same for all participants. There should be no elective studies. The student took what was deemed best for him, or left the place; he had no choice.

Hence there was no overlapping or reduplication of function anywhere along the line. The college, for example, did not reach back into the work of the secondary school to fill up any holes or take up any slack in the student's career there. If the student came to college unprepared in any particular, he was unprepared, and there was nothing to do about it but to remand him. No more did the college reach forward into the purview of the university or the technical school with any pre-vocational or pre-professional exercises. Each institution kept strictly to the doings in its own bailiwick, as a unit in a general system.

Such, I say, is the traditional way in which the mechanism of an educational system is supposed to work; and such, speaking broadly and with regard to the force of circumstances, was the way that our mechanism was set up to work. The progress through school and college did, in fact, remain quite strictly disciplinary up to the revolutionary period which set in, as well as one can put a date to it, about thirty-five years ago. Now, it was of the very essence of this disciplinary character—

the very fifth essence, as a mediævalist might say —that all the knowledge canvassed in these fixed curricula should be of the order known as formative. Instrumental knowledge, knowledge of the sort which bears directly on doing something or getting something, should have no place there; it should have as strict an institutional quarantine raised against it as cities raise against a plague. This discrimination was quite carefully regarded in our institutions until the revolution of thirty-five years ago broke it down. I suggest that we look for a moment at the disciplinary fixed curricula made up of purely formative studies, to see what it actually came to in practice.

Let us look at it in this way: let us suppose that an educable person found good schools and a good college, where all circumstances were favourable—there were such—what would he do, and what might be expected of him? After the three Rs, or rather for a time in company with them, his staples were Latin, Greek and mathematics. He took up the elements of these two languages very early, and continued at them, with arithmetic and algebra, nearly all the way through the primary, and all the way through the secondary schools. Whatever else he did, if anything, was inconsiderable except as related to these major subjects; usually some readings in classical history, geography and mythology. When he reached the undergraduate college at the age of sixteen or so, all his language-difficulties with Greek and Latin were forever behind him; he could read anything in either tongue, and write in either, and he was thus prepared to deal with both literatures purely as literature, to bestow on them a purely literary interest. He had also in hand arithmetic, and algebra as far as quadratics. Then in four years at college he covered practically the whole range of Greek and Latin literature; mathematics as far as the differential calculus, and including the mathematics of elementary physics and astronomy; a brief course, covering about six weeks, in formal logic; and one as brief in the bare history of the formation and growth of the English language.

What was the purpose of this? We may admit, I presume, the disciplinary value of these studies, since that has never been seriously disputed, so far as I know, but we may say a word, perhaps, about their formative character. The literatures of Greece and Rome comprise the longest and fullest continuous record available to us, of what the human mind has been busy about in practically every department of spiritual and social activity; every department, I think, except one—music. This record covers twenty-five hundred consecutive years of the human mind's operations in poetry, drama, law, agriculture, philosophy, architecture, natural history, philology, rhetoric, astronomy, politics, medicine, theology, geography, everything. Hence the mind that has attentively canvassed this record is not only a disciplined mind but an *experienced* mind; a mind that instinctively views any contemporary phenomenon from the vantage-point of an immensely long perspective attained through this profound and weighty experience of the human spirit's operations. If I may paraphrase the words of Emerson, this discipline brings us into the feeling of an immense longevity, and maintains us in it. You may perceive at once, I think, how different would be the view of contemporary men and things, how different the appraisal of them, the scale of values employed in their measurement, on the part of one who has undergone this discipline and on the part of one who has not. These studies, then, in a word, were regarded as formative because they are *maturing*, because they powerfully inculcate the views of life and the demands on life that are appropriate to maturity and that are indeed the specific marks, the outward and visible signs, of the inward and spiritual grace of maturity. And now we are in a position to observe that the establishment of these views and the direction of these demands is what is traditionally meant, and what we citizens of the republic of letters now mean, by the word *education;* and the constant aim at inculcation of these views and demands is what we know under the name of the Great Tradition of our republic.

An educational system was set up in our country, and lavishly endowed in response to the noble sentiment of parents for the advancement of their children. It was to be equalitarian, as the average man understood equality; that is to say, everybody should be regarded as able to take in its benefits. It should be democratic, as the average man understood democracy; that is to say, no one had any natural right to anything that everybody could not get. Very well, then, we said, education, traditionally, is the establishment of certain views of life and the direction of certain demands on life, views and demands which take proper account of the fundamental instincts of mankind, all in due measure and balance; the instinct of workmanship, the instinct of intellect and knowledge, of religion and morals, of beauty and poetry, of social life and manners. The aim at an inculcation of these views and demands is the Great Tradition of a truly civilised society. The traditional discipline, the process which has been found most competent to the purpose, is that chiefly of scrutinising the longest available continuous record of what the human mind has hitherto done with those instincts; what it has made out of them; what its successes and failures have been; and what is to be learned from both. Bring on your children, and we will put them through this process under the sanction of an equalitarian and democratic theory.

It did not work. We discovered almost at once that it did not work, and that apparently there was no way of making it work. The reason it did not work was that this process postulated an educable person, and everybody is not educable. Far from it, we discovered that relatively very few are educable, very few indeed. There became evident an irreconcilable disagreement between our equalitarian theory and the fact of experience. Our theory assumed that all persons are educable; our practical application of it simply showed that the Creator, in His wisdom and in His loving-kindness, had for some unsearchable reason not quite seen His way to fall in with our theory, for He had not made all persons educable. We found to our discomfiture that the vast majority of mankind have neither the force of intellect to apprehend the processes of education, nor the force of character to make an educational discipline prevail in their lives.

Thus we were faced with a serious dilemma.

THE THEORY OF EDUCATION

On the one side was our equalitarian theory, with all the power of a strong sentiment behind it, pushing it on into the test of practice. On the other side was the fact that an inscrutable Providence had most signally failed to do its part towards enabling our theory to stand this test. We had, then, the choice of revising our theory, or of letting it stand and sophisticating our practice into some sort of correspondence with it. If we let go of the equalitarian idea in our theory, the democratic idea would disappear with it; for if all persons are not educable, then some persons may pretend to a distinction to which all others may not pretend, whereby education becomes a kind of class-prerogative; and this is undemocratic.

We made our choice, leaving our theory unrevised and unexamined; it remains today the theory upon which our system undertakes to operate. I repeat for the sake of emphasis, that as far as I know, this theory has never been formally brought before the bar of letters for examination and critical judgment. Then, having made our choice, we set out at once on the business of overhauling, recasting, readjusting and tinkering the mechanics of our system; and this has gone on without cessation for thirty-five years, and so energetically as to degenerate at last into a mere panicky license of innovation. Plan after plan, method after method, programme after programme has been hailed and touted as the one thing needful, put into effect, carried on for a while, and then become outmoded in favour of some other; our shores are strewn with their wreckage—

Quæ regio in terris nostri non plena laboris?

VII

IN THE course of this procedure there came to pass the complete obliteration of a most important distinction which several writers have of late tried to revive, myself among them—I dealt with it in a brief essay published three years ago—the distinction between training and education. As we have observed, very few people are educable. The great majority remain, we may say, in respect of mind and spirit, structurally immature; therefore no amount of exposure to the force of any kind of instruction or example can ever determine in them the views of life or establish in them the demands on life, that are characteristic of maturity. You may recall the findings of the army tests; they created considerable comment when they were published. I dare say these tests are rough and superficial, but under any discount you think proper, the results in this case are significant. I do not remember the exact figures, but they are unimportant; the tests showed that an enormous number of persons of military age had no hope of ever getting beyond the average fourteen-year-old stage of development. When we consider what that average is, we are quite free to say that the vast majority of mankind cannot possibly be educated. They can, however, be trained; anybody can be trained. Practically any kind of mentality is capable of making some kind of response to some kind of training; and here was the salvation of our system's theory. If all hands would simply agree to call training education, to regard a trained person as an educated person and a training-school as an educational institution, we need not trouble ourselves about our theory; it was safe. Since everybody is trainable, the equalitarian side of our theory was safe. Since training in anything for anybody is a mere matter of money, equipment, and specific instruction, the democratic side of our theory was safe. Since a trained citizenry is equivalent to an educated citizenry, the patriotic aspect of our theory might have as much made of it as ever. Since, finally, opportunities for every conceivable kind of training might become abundant and cheap, in innumerable cases to be enjoyed for nothing, or nearly nothing, the parental sentiment in behalf of posterity was satisfied.

What we did, then, actually, was to make just this identification of training with education, and to reconstruct our system accordingly; and this was the revolution of thirty-five years ago. I do not say that at every step we were fully conscious of what we were doing, or of its implications and probable consequences; we proceeded, rather, as most revolutionists do, by a series of improvisations. We have been proceeding in that way ever since, and this too is characteristic of periods of attempted consolidation after a revolution. But that is what we actually did. The revolutionary principle was the identification of training with education; the revolutionary process was the summary sweeping away of the discipline set by the Great Tradition, and the construction of another procedure to replace it.

It may be remarked here that with the disappearance of the distinction between training and education, another distinction of great importance also disappeared, necessarily disappeared. I refer to the distinction between formative knowledge and instrumental knowledge. The discipline set by the Great Tradition concerned itself exclusively with formative knowledge. To justify replacing this discipline with another procedure which concerned itself chiefly with instrumental knowledge, as the procedure of training must obviously do, it became convenient to maintain that the distinction between these two orders of knowledge was quite artificial, that instrumental studies were in themselves formative, as much so as any, and altogether to be preferred on this account as well as on all others. Nothing worth having was to be gained by the intensive study of Greek and Roman literature, classical history, mathematics and formal logic, that could not be gained to better purpose by the study, say, of modern languages, English and the sciences. The revolutionary spirit had its way so completely that this distinction at once faded out of sight, and at present, probably, most of the younger spirits among us are quite unaware that it was ever drawn.

THE THEORY OF EDUCATION

As is the case with all revolutions, great general dissatisfaction put a powerful weapon in the hands of the revolutionists. The product of our system was poor, as a rule, and, as again is always the case in such circumstances, nobody was much interested in getting at the real reasons why it was poor, but rather to pitch upon the first thing in sight and take it as a ground of complaint. The great question thus became, What is the use of sheer mathematics, of sheer Greek and Latin? The question, too, was put with an animus that precluded anything like reasonable consideration, because collisions of opinion occurred and people became ruffled. The fact of the matter was that we had been trying to make a great many persons bear a discipline that they were distinctly unable to bear; the discipline was appropriate only to educable persons, and they were ineducable. Our educational theory required us to attempt this impossibility, and the results were what might be expected even if we had been administering that discipline to the best advantage, which for reasons that I have already cited, we were not always able to do.

IN THE UNITED STATES

But all this did not count. Dissatisfaction pitched upon the first thing in sight, the discipline itself, declared it worthless and insisted on its being done away.

In making up a procedure to replace the discipline of the Great Tradition, we were accidentally affected by certain social phenomena appearing at this time, which struck us with all the force of novelty. One was the general preoccupation with natural science, brought about by an unprecedented irruption of invention and discovery. Science touched the popular sense of awe and wonder. In a memorable conflict with many of the dogmatic constructions of organised Christianity, it had come off easily first best; and this had immense popular significance, such significance as is hard for us now even to imagine. Men's minds were full of the marvels of science; their imaginations were busy with its alluring prospect of further marvels. Here, then, was something out of which to construct a procedure. Children should not grow up ignorant of these matters, they should be taught "something about" the natural sciences. This idea

THE THEORY OF EDUCATION

was plausible, none could have been more so, and considering the great general preoccupation with the wonders of invention and discovery, none could have been more acceptable.

Accepted it accordingly was, and our institutions began at once to deal in dilutions of various sciences. Our secondary schools and colleges began to deal in diluted chemistry, diluted botany, diluted biology, and so on; the sum coming to a quite impressive list. Now, the point worth remarking here is that this fell in extremely well with the conditions imposed by our theory, because everybody can do anything with these dilutions of science that anybody can do, and nobody can get anything more out of them than everybody can get. Regarded as educational pursuits, they thus amply satisfy the requirements of an equalitarian and democratic theory. They do so because they rest wholly upon evidence of the senses. I do not say that all science rests upon evidence of the senses—there is no need to raise that point—but only that these dilutions do, and that therefore they are accessible to an extremely low order of intelligence, and are easily taught. This feature of our curricula is that upon which Matthew Arnold showered such exquisite raillery in his description of the Lycurgus House Academy and its guiding spirit, Archimedes Silverpump, Ph.D.; and in the summary of the Lycurgus House curriculum as drawn up by the hand of Silverpump's old pupil, Mr. Bottles. In that half-page you will miss hardly a single stock phrase of the eager innovator of yesterday; and probably no better criticism on the worth of his endeavours was ever formulated than the one that is implicit in the words of Mr. Bottles:

"That will do for land and the Church," said Arminius. "And now let us hear about commerce." "You mean how was Bottles educated?" answered I. "Here we get into another line altogether, but a very good line in its way, too. Mr. Bottles was brought up at the Lycurgus House Academy, Peckham. You are not to suppose from the name of Lycurgus that any Latin and Greek was taught in the establishment; the name only indicates the moral discipline and the strenuous earnest character imparted there. As to the instruction, the thoughtful educator who was principal of the

THE THEORY OF EDUCATION

Lycurgus House Academy—Archimedes Silverpump, Ph.D., you must have heard of him in Germany—had modern views. 'We must be men of our age,' he used to say. 'Useful knowledge, living languages, and the forming of the mind through observation and experiment, these are the fundamental articles of my educational creed.' Or, as I have heard his pupil Bottles put it in his expansive moments after dinner (Bottles used to ask me to dinner till that affair of yours with him in the Reigate train): 'Original man, Silverpump! fine mind! fine system! None of your antiquated rubbish—all practical work—latest discoveries in science—mind kept constantly excited—lots of interesting experiments—lights of all colours—fizz! fizz! bang! bang! That's what I call forming a man!'"

Interest in vocationalism also affected the content of our new procedure. The teaching of science answered the innovator's demand that our system should be modern and up to date, that we should be "men of our time." Vocationalism answered his demand that education should be "a preparation for life." These two demands were the revolution's main fulcrum for ousting the earlier discipline. It was easy to say that the earlier discipline is mediæval and out of relation to modern life, for in a sense that is true; but it is true in a sense easily misunderstood and distorted. It was easy to say that this discipline sends out its votaries quite unprepared to meet the actual conditions of present-day living, for that also is true in a sense; it did not send them out with any direct, specific preparation for getting anything or for doing anything. This it never did, never pretended to do. A general preparation it did give an educable person, first by inculcating habits of orderly, profound and disinterested thought; and second, by giving him an immense amount of experienced acquaintance with the way the human mind had worked in all departments of its activity. But this benefit, besides being communicable only to a few, could easily be made to seem vague and illusory in competition with those held out by a programme of vocationalism. Moreover, the economic circumstances of the country threw a halo of great seriousness around vocationalism's programme. With the closing of the frontier in 1890 and the subsequent centralisation of economic control, the opportunities for individual initiative rapidly dwindled. The stratification of our society into a small owning and exploiting class and a propertyless labouring class became more clearly apparent than ever before, and this gave rise to a sense that time was pressing. It was borne in upon our public that if a person wished to get on in the world, he had to hurry up about it. Not only were his chances of getting into the owning and exploiting class becoming few and small, but his prospective hold on even a middle-class position was becoming most uncertain; and on the other hand, the likelihood of his sinking into the exploited and propertyless labouring class was increasing at an alarming rate. He had no time for more than a vocational training. The ensuing mass-movement towards our technical and vocational schools and the vocational departments of our universities confirmed us in our theory, and set us to work even harder at making our general system correspond as closely to our theory as ever we could. Our institutions became more than ever equalitarian in the popular sense, more than ever democratic; more faithfully than ever did they try "to give the people what they want." The result is seen in the impressive nation-wide exhibit of what Mr. Flexner calls "bargain-counter education" that is spread before us at the present time, not only by our universities, which were the special subject of Mr. Flexner's examination, but by our secondary schools, which were the subject of Mr. Learned's examination, and by our colleges.

Another matter is worth our notice as bearing upon this situation; that is, the curious popular veneration for mere size and numbers, and the resulting persuasion that bigness is the same thing as greatness. The United States has made itself known as the land where "big things are done in a big way," and has not much troubled itself, as a rule, by the question whether they were always worth doing. The sanction of bigness was sufficient. By force of this persuasion, a big school is a great school. The first question asked about an educational institution is, How many students has it? Here we see our theory again emerging. An institution pretending really to educate people who are really educable would have relatively few students, not only because there are relatively few educable persons, but because of what is known in economics as the law of diminishing returns. If it had a relatively large number of students, the fact would in itself be enough to raise the suspicion that it was not doing its work well. The presence of large numbers is in the nature of things a pretty fair measure of an institution's equalitarian and democratic character, in the popular sense of those terms, and of its concern with "bargain-counter education," which with equal justice and perhaps no less elegance, Mr. Flexner might have styled grab-bag education.

In one of Mr. Hoover's campaign-speeches, according to the newspapers, he congratulated the country on having ten times as many students as any other country, in what he called "its institutions of higher learning." His congratulations were accepted without thought or question; their hollowness was not exposed, so far as I know, by a single editorial article; even the opposition newspapers said nothing about it. Probably campaign-speeches are not taken very seriously; we have learned to judge them rather by their sound than by their sense. Yet my impression is that this incident tends somewhat to show how devoutly incurious our public is about its fetich of size and number. Otherwise surely it would have occurred to some one to say, "But this may not be at all a matter for congratulation. Perhaps it is quite the opposite. In itself, the fact of our having so large an institutional population means nothing either way. Everything surely depends on what the students are like, and what the institutions are like, and what the students do in the institutions, and what sort of folk they are when they come out. Tell us about these matters, and then we will say whether we are to be congratulated or not." Quite possibly indeed, for anything that Mr. Hoover's speech implied to the contrary, the other nations may be the ones to be congratulated, not ourselves. Mr. Hoover was, in short, making an interested appeal to an undiscriminating and irrational popular sentiment of veneration for sheer size, sheer number; and this is clap-trap.

VIII

WE MAY now take a rapid glance at the actual state of things which all these influences have combined to bring about. The procedure in the secondary school is perhaps sufficiently open to common observation so that we need say nothing about it here, leaving it for a remark or two later on some special point. Let us speak of the university and the undergraduate college. Traditionally, the university was an association of scholars, grouped in four faculties; Literature, Law, Theology and Medicine. When I say an association of scholars, I mean that it was not quite precisely what we understand by a teaching institution. The interest of the students was not the first interest of the institution. Putting it roughly, the scholars were busy about their own affairs, but because the Great Tradition had to be carried on from generation to generation, they allowed certain youngsters to hang about and pick up what they could; they

THE THEORY OF EDUCATION

lectured every now and then, and otherwise gave the students a lift when and as they thought fit. The point is that the whole burden of education lay on the student, not on the institution or on the individual scholar. Traditionally, also, the undergraduate college put the whole burden of education on the student. The curriculum was fixed, he might take it or leave it; but if he wished to proceed bachelor of arts, he had to complete it satisfactorily. Moreover, he had to complete it pretty well on his own; there was no pressure of any kind upon an instructor to get him through it, or to assume any responsibility whatever for his progress, or to supply any adventitious interest in his pursuits. The instructor usually did make himself reasonably helpful, especially in the case of those whom he regarded as promising, but it was no part of the institution's intention or purpose that he should transfer any of the actual burden of education from the student's shoulders to his own, or contribute anything from his own fund of interest in his subject by way of making up for any deficiency of interest on the part of the student. I ask you, with your permission, to remark this point particularly.

In speaking now of the present-day university, I shall cite the one of which I am a very humble and unconsidered member. I do this not because of its prominence, or because I can so conveniently lift some references to it from Mr. Flexner's recent book, and thus save trouble. I do it because one may always, as a matter of good taste, use oneself or one's own for purposes of illustration in cases where by any chance that kind of service might be thought disagreeable. To begin with, then, we have Mr. Butler the other day expounding, and in extremely fine rhetoric attempting to justify, what he calls "the newest type of university organisation and influence." Well, of course, if one wishes to call that type of organisation a university organisation, one may do so; and if one can induce others to regard it as a university organisation, one may also do that. It must be pointed out, however, that in so doing one acts very arbitrarily, even violently. This type of organisation is not a development, but something entirely different from the traditional type of university organisation; it is entirely different in structure, entirely different in intention, entirely different in function. In structure, the four "learned" Faculties have been superseded by all manner of "departments" and "schools." In intention, the newest type of university organisation and influence is not primarily that of an association of scholars, but that of an association, more or less loose and sprawling, of pedagogues, of persons on whom, as we shall shortly see, the whole burden of education has been shifted. In function, this type does not contemplate education, in the traditional sense of the word; it contemplates training. In fact, of all our institutions, the university gives perhaps the most conspicuous example of the complete working out of our general theory; it is perhaps the most conspicuous example of what a popular doctrine of equalitarianism and democracy comes to in practice.

The undergraduate college, however, is in this respect no great way behind the university. It has degenerated into a curiously anomalous affair, exhibiting changes in structure, intention and function, which correspond to those exhibited by the university. Its repertory—one is rather put to it to find a name for its schedule of organised pursuits —at one end reaches back far into the secondary school, and at the other reaches forward into the technical and vocational schools, while at the middle, apparently by way of lagniappe, but actually for reasons that we shall look into a little later, it carries on some kind of formal dealings with literature, chiefly English. I never think of an undergraduate college without being reminded of a story which I heard you, Mr. President,* tell in public twenty years ago, the story of an over-assiduous mother who insisted on her boy's eating some asparagus, on the notion that it was good for him. When asked how he liked it, he said mournfully that it tasted raw at one end and rotten at the other.

In support of this view of the modern undergraduate college, I may cite some observations made by Mr. Flexner. A student in Columbia Col-

* The late president of the University of Virginia, Mr. E. A. Alderman, who was presiding at the delivery of these Lectures.

lege (which is an undergraduate college controlled by Columbia University) a student may complete the requirements for a bachelor's degree by including in his course of study such matters as: the principles of advertising; the writing of advertising copy; advertising layouts; advertising research; practical poultry-raising; business English; elementary stenography; newspaper practice; reporting and copy-editing; feature-writing; book-reviewing; wrestling and self-defence. By availing himself of some sort of traffic-arrangement with a sister institution belonging to Columbia, he may also count as leading to a degree, courses in: the fundamental processes of cookery; fundamental problems in clothing; clothing decoration; family meals; food etiquette and hospitality; principles of home laundering; social life of the home; gymnastics and dancing for men, including practice in clog-dancing; instruction, elementary or advanced, in school orchestras and bands.

Without the least wish to be flippant, one cannot help remarking points of resemblance here between the newest type of institutional organisation and the newest type of drug-store. Perhaps the term "drug-store education" is even more closely descriptive than either Mr. Flexner's "bargain-counter education" or the term "grab-bag education," which I proposed a moment ago, for one goes to drug-stores nowadays for nearly everything but drugs. Really, this type is so new and so startling that no ready-made term fits it very well. But if one is thus somewhat at a loss in surveying the comprehensive prospectus of Columbia College, one simply throws up one's hands and capitulates before the advertised programme of another smaller undergraduate institution which, according to an announcement in the press, proposes to make up a special curriculum for each student, apparently a sort of hand-tailored affair, adapted to individual intentions, aptitudes and deficiencies. This strikes me as more than a counsel of despair; it is a counsel of desperation. Yet really, the only thing that differentiates this college from many other colleges, in this respect, is that it has the commendable forthrightness to say plainly what it means to do.

IX

YET, bearing in mind the terms of our general theory, one perceives at once that no other line of institutional development is practicable or possible, and one is therefore free from any imputation of ill-nature in remarking the kind of development that has actually taken place. Given the conditions of our theory, we have seen that our system is precisely such as one would expect; and we now see that our institutions are precisely such as one would expect. They cannot help themselves; their organisers and administrators cannot help themselves. So long as they choose to remain organisers or administrators, they must organise or administer under the prescription of an impossible and fantastic conception of equality, an impossible and fantastic conception of democracy; and the upshot of their efforts must be precisely such a system as we have, precisely such institutions as we have. There is an alternative, of course, but it is one that suggests itself at once and needs no comment;

it is rather exorbitant to expect them to take it, and in the long-run, probably, matters would be not much improved by their doing so. The most that can be expected, and also the least, is that they should be perfectly clear in their own minds about what they are doing, and never for a single moment persuade themselves that it is what it is not, or attempt to extenuate it or justify themselves in it on the strength of any such persuasion. In the realm of morals, I suspect that what one does is of much less importance than a failure in intellectual integrity concerning the nature of what one does. I have no need to remind you that the responsibility for continuous exercise of an absolutely spotless intellectual integrity rests most heavily upon those who pretend to be continuators of the Great Tradition. It is of the essence of the Great Tradition that the disinterestedness and objectivity implied in Plato's phrase should, first and last and most inflexibly, be maintained upon ourselves, our interests and desires, above all upon our ambitions and achievements. Let these be what they may; possibly better this than that, possibly finer, nobler, more in character with our pretensions as disciples of the Great Tradition, children of light—all that is for us to weigh and judge—but the important thing is that we should invariably see them as they are.

"The newest type of university organisation," then, we perceive to be essentially the same as the newest type of college organisation; and examination of our secondary-school organisation will show that also as essentially the same. Our institutional pattern runs the same throughout our system. Our institutions organise the identification of training with education; they organise the disregard of disciplinary processes and formative knowledge. They organise, precisely as M. Renan said, "a considerable popular instruction without any serious higher education." Under the influence of vocationalism and the fetich-worship of size and numbers, they have stuffed out the content of this popular instruction to an incredible volume. No institution could afford to be behind its neighbours in this; all alike had to have a hand in it, for such as did not would go to the wall. It is fair, I think, to say that our institutions have conducted among themselves a grand competition for numbers, on ruinous terms; first, by shifting the burden of education from the student to the instructor, and putting pressure on the instructor to let his students go through as lightly and quickly as possible; and second, by offering a choice among an immense number of subjects that are easily taught, and easily accessible to a very low order of mind.

In this connexion I have already mentioned the dilutions of various sciences. Looking over the list of subjects which Mr. Flexner cites as available to candidates for Columbia College's baccalaureate, you will acknowledge, I think, that the difficulties they present are chiefly mechanical. Research in cookery, for instance, home laundering, wrestling, are subjects not beyond comprehension by the average intellect, though a certain mechanical unhandiness might hold one back from proficiency in them. With these we may class, for our purposes, two pursuits that the newest type of institutional organisation does a great deal with; that is to say, modern languages and what is known as "courses in English." With regard to modern languages, we must make a discrimination that is perhaps seldom observed. A use, say, of Italian or French as a literary language, giving us full command of a great literature in addition to our own—this is one thing. A use which aims at conversation, or as Matthew Arnold said, enables us to fight the battle of life with the waiters in foreign hotels—this is quite another thing. It is the latter use which is in vogue in our institutions, because it is more easily taught and more easily appropriated. I was lately shown a dormitory in an undergraduate college, and was told that people spoke only French in that house, no other language being permitted. This did not interest me. I asked what they said when they spoke French, this being the only thing that counts, for one may chatter nonsense and inanities in French as well as in any other language, I suppose. I got no satisfaction on this point; yet it is most important. The one use of French may be arrived at through the other, no question; yet a quite complete possession of the second use is no guarantee that the other will be attained, and experience shows that it seldom is attained. The best linguists we know, using the word in our institutional sense, are persons who are intellectually quite incompetent to apply their proficiency to even the most rudimentary literary purposes. We all have seen commissionaires in Marseilles who speak half a dozen languages faultlessly, yet have no literary use of any of them and no power of acquiring such use. On the other hand, we know persons who speak French, say, most execrably, yet who know the history and structure of the language as few Frenchmen know it, and are as much at home in the archaic French of the fifteenth century—French that not one in a hundred Frenchmen can read—as they are in the French of the Academy, or of the Paris morning newspaper. Mr. Jefferson, you no doubt remember, never attempted to speak any language but English, except under great pressure; yet he had full command of the Italian and French literatures.

With regard to "courses in English," I suspect that if you have not already done some such thing, there is a surprise in store for you when you make an estimate of the number of them that our institutions offer annually. I suggest that you look into the matter, and meanwhile I shall not anticipate your findings, being desirous that they should make their own impression on you and carry their own intimations. I therefore say only that there are a great many such courses, whereas forty years ago no such thing was known. Why should this be so? Forty years ago, our English-speaking students learned English quite informally; it was our own tongue, we were bred to a native idiomatic use of it, such a use as none but a native can ever possibly acquire. To say that English was not taught in our higher institutions means merely that everybody taught it. No matter what the stated subject under discussion might be, if we expressed ourselves inaccurately, loosely, unidiomatically, we heard about it at once and on the spot, and in terms that forcibly suggested a greater carefulness in the future. As for English literature, it was our literature, our concern with it was proprietary, everything in it was open to us, and the critical judgment, the standards of taste and discrimination that we applied to it, were such as had been bred in us by our long acquaintance with the literatures of Greece and Rome. No one dreamed of *teaching* English literature; indeed, I do not see how it can be effectively taught in any formal fashion, how a really competent acquaintance with it can be brought about in any other way than the way by which it was brought about in us. Why, then, is it that "courses in English" should hold so large a place in the newest type of institutional organisation? They do so for a very simple reason. Under the conditions that we have been describing, great masses of ineducable people come into our institutions. They must be kept there, and must nominally be busy with something or other as a *pro forma* justification for keeping them. Therefore something has to be found for them to do that they can do, and this is a hard matter because they can do almost nothing. One thing they can do, albeit after a very poor fashion, is to read; that is to say, they can make their way more or less uncertainly down a printed page; and therefore "courses in English" have come into their present extraordinary vogue. Well, here is a small garland of windflowers culled by an instructor from the work, not of primary-school children, but of university students, chiefly upper-class men, who were busy with "courses in English":

> "Being a tough hunk of meat, I passed up the steak."
> "Lincoln's mind growed as his country kneaded it."
> "The camel carries a water tank with him; he is also a rough rider and has four gates."
> "As soon as music starts silence rains, but as soon as it stops it get worse than ever."
> "College students, as a general rule, like such readings that will take the least mental inertia."
> "Modern dress is extreme and ought to be checked."
> "Although the Irish are usually content with small jobs they have won a niche in the backbone of the country."

The instructor who reported these efforts went on to show how Shakespeare fared at the hands of their authors:

> Edmund in *King Lear* "committed a base act and allowed his illegitimate father to see a forged letter." Cordelia's death "was the straw that broke the camel's

THE THEORY OF EDUCATION

back and killed the king." Lear's fool "was prostrated on the neck of the king." "Hotspur," averred a sophomore, "was a wild, irresolute man. He loved honour above all. He would go out and kill twenty Scotchmen before breakfast." Kate was "a woman who had something to do with hot spurs."

Also Milton:

"Diabetes was Milton's Italian friend," one student explained. Another said: "Satan had all the emotions of a woman and was a sort of trustee in heaven, so to speak." The theme of *Comus* was given as "purity protestriate." Mammon in *Paradise Lost* suggests that the best way "to endure hell is to raise hell and build a pavilion."

The newest type of institutional organisation has obliterated the lines that formerly marked off the units of our system and bounded their respective bailiwicks. Each unit is doing a little of everything, a little secondary-school work, a little college work, a little vocational work, and what not. Certain new units also have been knaved up out of this hodge-podge to do likewise a little of everything; the "junior college," for example. Some years ago I visited an old acquaintance in the

Middle West, who was teaching English in a huge swollen institution that went by the name of a State university. I looked in on one of my friend's classes in "English composition," and found him engaged on a kind of thing that by the very handsomest concession was only eighth-grade work; and his students were dealing with it in a manner that an educable eighth-grade pupil would regard as disgraceful. These students were not eighth-grade pupils; they were adult persons, ranking *bona fide* as part of a university population, and eligible for a degree authorised by a university.

The outcome of our theory in this particular may be clearly seen by another reference to the undergraduate college, as occupying a middle ground among our institutions. Not long ago I visited an undergraduate college—not one of those connected with Columbia University—and on casually looking into matters there, I told the president that I was surprised to see the college doing so much work that belonged far back in the grade school. He said it was unfortunate, but it could not be helped; students came there with these holes in their preparation that had to be filled up. I observed that the undergraduate college was perhaps hardly in a position to afford these diversions from its proper business, and that it seemed likely to suffer from them. "Yes," he said, "but don't you think we ought to do *something* for these poor fellows who come to us so imperfectly prepared?"

"Certainly I do," I said. "Fire them."

"Ah, yes," he replied, "but then, you see, we should not have any students and would have to shut up shop."

I hinted as delicately as I could that this might not be in the long-run an absolute misfortune; as I remember, I may have quoted Homer's pertinent line on the death of Patroclus. He admitted the force of this, but said, "We are doing a poor job, I know, but we are doing something as best we can, and I think a little better than most institutions of our kind; so we hope it is worth while."

At the other end of the line, this college was doing quite a thriving business in pre-professional and pre-vocational training. Having asked about this, I was told that the lads were in a hurry to get

IN THE UNITED STATES

on with their vocations and did not feel like spending time on any work that had not a direct vocational bearing; if such work were insisted on, they would simply leave, and go to some other place where the requirements were more generous. Here you may quite see what it is that obliterates the lines between the units of our system, and also where the responsibility for that obliteration and its consequences really lies. If you will permit the expression, the college passes the buck to the secondary school; and there is a measure of justice in that. The school, also with a measure of justice, replies, "If you are not satisfied with the way these men are prepared, why do you admit them? We cannot consider your requirements alone; we have very many diverse demands made on us, and must do the best we can to meet all of them." The vocational or technical school, the office or the factory —post-collegiate conditions generally—say to the college, "We cannot altogether accommodate ourselves to your ideas; if these young men are in such a pucker to get on in the world, it is your business to start them right, according to the conditions that actually exist"; and there is a measure of justice in that, too. Responsibility, clearly, lies nowhere in the order of our institutions; it runs back to the acceptance of an erroneous theory. All this ludicrous state of things that we have been examining is the inevitable result of trying to translate a bad theory into good practice.

Certain other aspects of this state of things are worth a moment's notice, in order that we may see how directly they come about in consequence of the attempt to turn bad theory into good practice. Granted our theory, they could be forecast and postulated as inevitable. A system constructed on this theory must comprise an immense amount of machinery, and as we have seen, so long as the theory is kept to, this machinery will be incessantly multiplied, overhauled and tinkered in the vain hope of making it work better than it can. Thus our system invites, nay, we may almost say commands, the interest of persons whose approach to it is most undesirable; the careerist, adventurer, quidnunc, hand-over-head experimenter, publicity-getter, profiteer and quack. It is not to our pur-

IN THE UNITED STATES

pose to inquire how far the administration of our system is actually in the hands of gentry such as these; we merely remark the fact, about which there can be no doubt, that a system erected on our theory is most freely and conspicuously liable to their incursions. Moreover, it is notorious that a period of attempted consolidation after a revolution always opens the way for the ascendency of elements that are in every respect objectionable; and hence on both these grounds our system occupies an extremely vulnerable position.

Then, too, the erection and operation of this vast amount of machinery has tended quite strictly to formalise its administration; and this in turn has tended to the disappearance of individuals whose gifts, abilities and distinctions were not of the order prescribed by a rigidly formalised routine, but were nevertheless very useful. You are aware, of course, that the older type of institutional organisation made a great place for such individuals. In the Middle Ages, the association of educable persons with them, and the exposure to the spiritual influences that they generated, pretty well made up all there was to education. Here or there would emerge some great man, like Peter Abélard, John of Scotland, Bernard of Clairvaux, and aspiring youngsters out of all peoples, nations and languages would lay down the shovel and the hoe, pack up some provisions, tramp off and find them, camp down with them and pick up what they had to give; then tramp off to the next man whom they had heard of as mounting pretty heavy guns, and then the next. If you have not done so, I venture to suggest that you read Miss Helen Waddell's scholarly, unpretentious and exquisitely sympathetic little book on the *Vagantes*, the wandering students of the Middle Ages. Do not be afraid of it, I am not trying to make mediævalists of you, you may read and enjoy it and still remain "men of your time." I merely suggest that the view of another type of educational routine, albeit one that our system disallows, is interesting. Some vestiges of this routine survived well into our own time. You will notice that nowadays a person always says, I am a graduate of Virginia, or of Columbia, or of Harvard, and lets it go at that. I myself can remember when one seldom heard a person speak so. I can distinctly remember a time when the regular way, the natural and instinctive way, to put it, was, I studied under Mr. Humphreys, or Mr. John B. Minor, or Mr. Gildersleeve, or Mr. Frank Smith, at the University of Virginia. The man was instinctively brought first to mind, and put in the place of honour, and in honouring the man one honoured the institution that maintained him. Precisely so in the first half of the sixteenth century, you find one of Rabelais's characters saying, "When I was a law-student at Poitiers under *Brocardium Juris*," this being a student's nickname for one of the law-professors at the University of Poitiers, possibly Robert Irland, or Ireland, a Scotsman who taught law there for fifty years, and did much to make the Faculty of Law at Poitiers one of the most distinguished in all Europe. Rabelais also has Panurge make a playful reference to some readings under "the most decretalipotent Scotch doctor" at Poitiers, which this time almost certainly points to Robert Irland. He also

THE THEORY OF EDUCATION

has Pantagruel going the customary round of the French universities, as Rabelais himself may have done, judging by the casual record of his acquaintance with distinguished men connected with some of them: Boyssonné at Toulouse, Schyron and Rondellet at Montpellier, and so on. The point is that all these men were (if I may put it so without offence; I certainly mean none) distinguished for something that lies outside the scope of a pedagogy established on trade-unionist principles. In our own country, many years ago, when the Great Tradition was respected among us, and its discipline as well as possible maintained, the authorities at Harvard thought it worth while to keep Oliver Wendell Holmes demonstrating anatomy, Longfellow teaching (I think) Spanish, and James Russell Lowell teaching Romance languages. Technically, I dare say there were better men available for these specialties, and certainly in the trade-unionist sense, Holmes, Longfellow and Lowell had no qualifications worth speaking of. But they were completely and conspicuously in the Great Tradition, they were children of light. All their works and ways had the mark of the Great Tradition upon them, not the mark of Dagon. Therefore any mode of association with them, whether over Spanish, or anatomy, or what you will, continually liberated the Great Tradition's influence, spread the contagion of its charm, and powerfully recommended its discipline; and this, in the view of the older type of institutional organisation, made them abundantly worth their keep.

As evidence tending to show the difference between this view and the view of the newer type of organisation, I may mention a recent experience of my own with one of the best philologists in the country. Somewhere in his sphere of influence there had turned up a boy who in earlier days would have passed muster as a good promising student, nothing to get excited about, but who now was to be regarded as something of a prodigy in Greek and Latin studies. He had got about all he could get where he was, and the question was what to do with him. Did I know of any outstanding man in any institution anywhere in America, with whom he could be put; any man who was at all notably a continuator of the Great Tradition? My interlocutor, a man of my own age, and I looked at each other in silence for about twenty minutes while we overhauled all the resources of our memory, and then had to give up. We could think off-hand of excellent technicians, well-trained reporters, and all that sort of thing, but that was as far as we could go. We then remarked the strangeness of the fact—for it did seem strange when looked at in retrospect from the present state of things—that thirty years ago we could have rattled you off the names of a dozen or more in a moment, as fast as our tongues could run.

Another interesting feature of this present condition of affairs is the complete disappearance of what may be called the non-professional scholar, such as foreign countries have always produced, and still produce, and of which we ourselves formerly produced a few, some of them quite notable. One of the best Latinists in England of the last generation was a bishop; one of the very best Greek scholars in England was the head of the huge Westminster Bank. Some of England's public men of the period, like Mr. Asquith and Mr. Gladstone, were good scholars. Even now, among France's public men, M. Poincaré is an excellent man of letters. At the height of the war M. Poincaré, representing the French Academy at the centenary of Ernest Renan, wrote an appreciation of Renan's position in the world of letters that was redolent of good sound literary learning and taste; and M. Barthou did as much in his capacity as representing the Institute of Science on the same occasion. In our own country, the revision of our standard Latin lexicon was made almost entirely by a man in the insurance business. The history of the Inquisition which has held the field undisputed for thirty years was written by a retired publisher in Philadelphia. A newspaper editor gave us our best translation of a Greek historian. Bearing our theory in mind, you will have no trouble about seeing that this sort of thing was bound to disappear as promptly and completely as it has. With education supplanted by training, and vocationalism rampant, it could not do otherwise. One of the most interesting and significant assumptions in the world is that which you will nowadays encounter everywhere in American society: if a person shows signs of having an education, properly so called, the assumption is almost invariably, first, that he got it in Europe, and second, that he makes his living by it or at least uses it for purposes of profit. This, I repeat, is most significant. I am strongly tempted to trace out some of its implications, but what has been said already will probably make them apparent.

It may be said—indeed, it is often said—that this is an age of science, and that we have men of science who are as eminent and influential as those whom we have just cited. If Harvard, for example, no longer has a Holmes and a Lowell, this means no more than that their places have been taken by Mr. X., the biologist, and Mr. Y., the physicist, who are quite as eminent as Holmes and Lowell were, quite as highly regarded and as much looked up to. While we may freely accept this statement as it stands, two things are to be noted. First, eminence in science does not necessarily imply eminence in the Great Tradition, and eminence in the Great Tradition is what we are talking about. A man may be most eminent, for instance, in the science of medicine, he may be the most skilful practitioner living, or the most capable man in research, or whatever else you will, without bearing anything remotely resembling the mark of the Great Tradition. One may be ever so eminent as a physicist, yet with an eminence wholly different from that which distinguished some physicists of the last generation who notably bore this mark. We may go further than this. A man may even be most eminent on the scientific side of the Great Tradition's discipline itself, he may be thoroughly up on its whole technique, and yet be in no sense a continuator of the Great Tradition. On the contrary, his views of life and his demands on life may be such as show conclusively that he is all abroad in it, quite untouched by its formative power. To say this is no more than to remark what is a matter of common observation, that an ineducable person may succeed in training himself in the sheer science of the Great Tradition's discipline, and remain none the less ineducable. Not long ago, I remember, I was looking over a volume of minor Greek verse which on the scientific side was a marvel of editing, but that was all one could say for it; one laid it down with gratitude that one had escaped an introduction to Greek literature at the editor's hands.

Our reply is, then, that we are not interested in eminence except of a special order. Let us have all the science there is, of course—one can never have too much—but stark eminence in science does not in the present instance command our interest. The object of education, as we understand the word, the purpose of enforcing the Great Tradition's discipline, is to inculcate certain views of life and certain demands on life. Hence this object is not to produce, say, great practitioners of medicine, but (if you will permit me to bring forward some examples by name) to produce great practitioners like Pancoast and William Osler. Not to produce great physicists, but great physicists like Mr. Millikan. Not great philologists and grammarians, but those like Gildersleeve and Humphreys, who had all the science there was, but who employed it in all their works and ways for the furtherance of the Great Tradition, and for that alone.

The second observation which we must make concerning the eminence of men of science in our day and country, is one that we may not perhaps care to dwell on too closely, but undoubtedly we should remind ourselves that by reason of the rather questionable principles upon which publicity is organised among us, a person may be eminent and not be conspicuous. His eminence may be duly acknowledged in all quarters where such acknowledgement counts for anything, and he may yet remain otherwise almost unknown. It is only by a certain order of achievement in science that he becomes conspicuous; that is to say, if he invents or discovers something that can be popularised, like the telephone, or if he writes popularly on some subject that touches the curiosity of a large public, as Sir James Jeans is doing, or if, like Mr. Einstein, his pursuits are such as are exploitable by journalism. One may doubt that the names of Dana, Gray and even Agassiz were as well known in their day, or are now as well known, as those of Morse and Bell; yet there is no question about their eminence. In the last generation, this country produced one of the most eminent men of science in the whole world. His name was quite unknown among us while he lived, and it is still unknown. Yet I may say without too great exaggeration that when I heard it mentioned in a professional assembly in the Netherlands two years ago, everybody got down under the table and touched their foreheads to the floor. His name was Josiah Willard Gibbs.

Now, the object of this observation is not to intimate that spurious or inflated reputations are easily made among us; whether this be true to any great extent or not is no concern of ours at the moment. We may raise the question, however, whether the general interest in science which as a people we are supposed to have, actually exists. It is taken for granted, especially by unfriendly critics of the Great Tradition's discipline, that as a people we are of a scientific turn, and have great interest in science. I see no reason to believe this.

IN THE UNITED STATES

We are greatly interested in the practical outcome of invention and discovery; that is clear, and we need not go too far out of our way to attribute a mercenary motive to this interest. We are also, I think, greatly possessed of an indolent, passive and fitful curiosity about certain superficial and speculative concerns of science, which causes us to skim their large popular literature with some frail and tenuous semblance of attention. We are also susceptible to sensation-mongering, such as that which poor Mr. Einstein found so ready to be visited on him when he came here; a most discreditable and repulsive performance on the part of our journalists who, as you no doubt remember, drew on the very last resources of their loathsome profession in the effort to exploit his superb achievements. But that we have, as for instance the Germans so notably have, an ingrained regard for science, an instinctive respect for whatever is *wissenschaftlich*, a sense that there is a right and a wrong way of doing things, and that the right way is the one to be followed—this is in my judgment rather more than doubtful, for I nowhere see evidence of the working of any such spirit. Therefore when it is assumed that this turn for science has anything to do with a disparagement of the Great Tradition's discipline, I would suggest that we examine carefully the premises of this assumption before we accept it.

X

WE ARE now in a position, probably, to deal with the little problem which we set ourselves awhile ago, and which for convenience we may now restate. Why is it that our post-revolutionary conditions seem no more satisfactory than our pre-revolutionary conditions? We have done everything to our system that ingenuity can devise and that money can pay for; why, then, does it work no better in point of produce than it ever did? What is the meaning of the general chorus of complaint about it, and what are the specific bearings, the "indications," as the physicians say, of surveys like those of Mr. Learned, Mr. Flexner, and others? Is it not clear that the whole difficulty lies with the theory upon which we are trying to erect a workable system? Is it not clear also that so long as we persist with an unsound theory, we never can, by any exercise of ingenuity, set up a system that will work any better than ours is now working?

THE THEORY OF EDUCATION

I think there can be no doubt about it. Earlier in these Lectures, you may remember, I suggested a comparison between the product of the Continental university and ours. Compare the material resources, the "plant" and equipment, of, say, a French provincial university and one of ours; and then compare the general run of produce. In this year of depression, sixty-five of our institutions report themselves as proposing to spend $62,500,000 on building alone. Looking at a Continental university and at what comes out of it, one may very seriously ask, What for? By comparison with the "plant" which I see around me here at the University of Virginia, the great University of Bonn, which is in the very aristocracy of German universities, looks like a barrack. What would be the emotions of a really up-to-date, live-wire, go-getting American university-president (I venture to use these terms because in this particular connexion they seem to have passed out of the glossary of slang and into conventional good usage) if he were invited to Poitiers or Montpellier and went to take a look around his new domain? Yet see the produce that comes out of Bonn, Poitiers, Montpellier, and then see what comes out of ours!

The root of the matter is, I repeat, that the Continental institution has no false and fantastic conceptions of equality and democracy to which it must conform, and no inflated notion of the social value of a literate citizenry. We in the United States hear a great deal about the "average student," and his capacities, needs and desires. The Continental institution feels under no obligation to regard the average student as a privileged person. He is there on his own, if he be there at all, and he finds nothing cut to his measure, no organised effort to make things easy and pleasant for him, no special consideration for his deficiencies, his infirmity of purpose, or the amount or quality of intellectual effort that he is capable of making. Equality and democracy enjoin no such responsibility on these institutions. In the Prussian schools, modelled on the Crown Patronage Schools, you will indeed see the shoemaker's son sitting between the banker's son and the statesman's son, over the same lessons; but equality and democracy,

THE THEORY OF EDUCATION

as we popularly understand them, have nothing to do with this. The three boys sit there because they are able to do the work, and it matters not which one of the three, if any, finds it too hard going, and drops out. The upshot of the Continental system's freedom from unsound notions about equality and democracy is that its processes are selective; "the best geniuses," as Mr. Jefferson said, are diligently "raked from the rubbish," and the rubbish is not suffered to clog the workings of the system's machinery. Our system, on the contrary, is engaged with the rubbish, because the theory of its operation requires it to be so engaged.

Now, since hardly any one is satisfied with the way our system is working, let us see for a moment what the precise grounds are for complaint against it. Suppose we had the reorganization and re-direction of it wholly in our hands, just what changes would we make? It may possibly surprise you a little to hear me say that I would make hardly any actual changes, and those I would make are only such as should enable our system to go on doing practically what it is doing now, but to do it better. Our dissatisfaction, really, is due only to some vague notion that we ought to be gathering grapes from thorns or figs from thistles. The case therefore, in my judgment, is one that calls for clarification of thought, in the first instance, and when that has taken place, it will be seen that the actual changes in our system which are indicated by clear thought are few and simple. Clear thought, to begin with, reëstablishes the distinction between education and instruction or training. Then, since experience shows that the great majority, though quite ineducable, are capable of being trained, it seems to me that our system's line of development is essentially the right one. There is, obviously, a great social advantage in having a trained citizenry, as there is in having a literate citizenry; but in both cases the advantage is not what we thought it was, but something quite different. There is no political advantage, such as Mr. Jefferson imagined, in having a literate citizenry; experience, I should say, has established this beyond doubt; but an artisan, for example, who can read a slip of printed directions is more of a social asset than one who cannot, for he makes less trouble for other people in getting the hang of his work. Similarly, though the actual civilisation of a society does not especially profit if the ineducable majority are given all the instruction they can take in, its material well-being is in a way to be considerably advanced thereby, and the sum of its happiness is no doubt in a way to be somewhat increased. I speak thus cautiously because this outcome, as you know, depends wholly on the kind of economic system that the society has in force. Under one kind of system, indeed, a trained citizenry may be only the more profitably exploitable in virtue of this superior training, and the advantage in material well-being may thus accrue only the more largely to a small owning and exploiting class. But with due allowance made for these circumstances, one may say broadly that a society is better off for having its ineducables as well trained as they are capable of becoming.

Well, then, here surely is the argument for vocationalism; it is a perfectly sound one, so why not accept it instead of wasting time over others which are not sound, but are on the contrary, quite specious? Here is the ground of justification for the "new million-dollar high school," for Mr. Butler's new type of institutional organisation, and for an extension of the elective plan clear to the logical limit of the bargain-counter, grab-bag or drug-store policy. Let us be quite serious about this. There are two distinct points of view. Hitherto we have been considering our system and its institutional life from the point of view of *education*. Now we are considering them from the point of view of *instruction* or *training*. If in the first instance we are perfectly clear in our minds about what it is we wish to do—that is, to train to the best advantage a vast number of ineducable persons—really, is not our system, in all essential respects, pretty well organised to do it, and are not our institutions giving a fairly good account of themselves in point of results? I think so. Then if this be admitted, can any one suggest anything more to the purpose than that our system should remain virtually as it is, and that our institutions should go on doing what they are doing now? I think it very doubtful.

For my own part, if my attention were officially invited to the matter, I should have but two suggestions to offer. At present, our institutions, all the way through the system, feel a certain responsibility, over and above their function as training-schools, for doing as much with education as under their very untoward circumstances they are able to do. This is a great disability, and it should be removed. It is imposed on them only by unclear thinking, as we may see by a moment's glance at their actual situation. We set up an institution, load it to the gunwales with ineducable persons, proceed to train them in brick-laying, dish-washing, retail shoe-merchandising, or what not, and then insist that there should be somewhere a poor pennyworth of bread thrown in with this intolerable deal of sack. Mr. Butler says that the results accruing to our processes are "admitted to be anything but satisfactory." But from what point of view? Certainly not from that of the actual intention of the system, of the institution. The only question, really, is whether the persons trained in the institution turn out good bricklayers, shoe-salesmen, dish-washers. If they do—and I am not in a position to say whether they do or not—then I submit that the new type of institutional organisation has done all that can be expected of it, and is entitled to a clean bill. From the point of view of *education*—the point of view that we have hitherto taken—Mr. Butler's observation is sound beyond peradventure. But under the circumstances is it competent for him to take that point of view? I cannot see that it is.

It was this thought that prompted my playful reply to my Italian friend, whose comment I mentioned at the outset of these Lectures. He, like Mr. Butler, was vaguely expecting our system to produce something that it is not organised to produce and cannot possibly produce, and was vaguely disappointed at finding no such product. Judged by its intention, I should say, as I said to my Italian friend, that it is doing extremely well; and I suggest that it should be relieved of any responsibility beyond its intention. If the press reports are true, Mr. Henry Ford, in his school for boys at Sudbury, has worked out a plan that seems to correspond exactly with the suggestion that I am making. He takes boys in—presumably all ineducable, as none other would see any reason for going there—and trains them in purely instrumental knowledge with never a grain of formative knowledge from first to last. In this I think he is precisely right; and I venture to think that just this is what all our institutions should be doing, and that a great many more institutions should be set up to do the same thing, for the ineducable are among us as the sands of the sea for multitude.

The other suggestion that I would make is that having thus dropped all pretence to an educational character, our system and its institutions should drop all titles, like that of *college* and *university*, which by age-long usage intimate this character. Our system is not educational; we have seen that its fundamental theory makes it impossible to attribute any such character to it. Its institutions are not educational institutions. Why, then, should there be any pretence to the contrary? Nobody, I think, could say more in praise of Mr. Butler's newer type of institutional organisation than I have just now said. Nobody could be more cordially in favour of it than I am. Yet I repeat that there is great violence and great impropriety in describing it as a university organisation; great violence, in wresting a very old title quite away from anything remotely resembling its traditional significance; and great impropriety, by consequence, in exposing the public, always careless in such matters, to the risk of most serious misapprehension. I noticed the other day in a French newspaper a quotation from the dean of Harvard University's School of Business Administration. The writer was puzzled, as well he might be, about this novel and anomalous designation, and finally compromised with his conscience by putting the title in quotation-marks, and calling this dignitary the dean of the Faculty of "*Affaires.*" It seems to me that this trifling incident puts the matter in a clear light. There is nothing in the world wrong with a school of business administration. We ought to have a great many of them, and make them all as good as we can; they are invaluable. But a school of business administration existing as a university Faculty is an inadmissible anomaly, quite as this French editorial writer perceived it to be. Let me take every pains to avoid misunderstanding. The institution with which I am connected is doing a good and great work, a necessary work, and doing it extremely well. Mr. Butler's ideas of this work, as set forth in his last presidential address are, I think, beyond the reach of cavil or question. If I had my way, I would set up institutions on the same model all over the land. But I think it is most unjustifiable to call this institution a university, because by age-long use-and-wont the title conveys a wholly erroneous notion of the institution's character and activities. Surely there is nothing discreditable, say, about the name *institute;* it is in good usage everywhere, and carries just the right notion of what now goes on under the name of university work. As far as I know, there does not exist a university or an undergraduate college, in the traditional and proper sense, anywhere in the country. I cannot see that there would be any

IN THE UNITED STATES

conceivable sacrifice of prestige if our institutions honourably and scrupulously gave up a title to which they have but a most questionable right, and called themselves institutes. There is plenty of good precedent for this. The Royal Institute, the *Istituto Fisico*, the Institute of Science, in our own country the Renssalaer Polytechnic Institute, your Virginia Polytechnic Institute at Blacksburg, the Massachusetts Institute of Technology, the Stevens Institute, the Rice Institute—the title is an honourable one, and deceives no one by the implication of an improper pretence.

My suggestion would include the suppression of meaningless and misleading individual academic titles as well as institutional titles. As Mr. Flexner has pointed out, there is something monstrous and shocking about the conferring of an academic degree in the liberal arts, on the strength of such qualifications as he cites—wrestling, poultry-raising, advertising research, clothing decoration, and so on. Mr. Flexner has spoken so well and forcefully of this unnatural proceeding that I can add nothing to what he has said. If I should come here and try to impress you by saying that my institution turned out so-many hundred Masters of Arts last year, and would turn out so-many hundred more this year, I should expect you to reply somewhat thus: "Yes, that is all very fine, very good, but what are they like? To bear the degree of Master of Arts is an immense pretension, and *noblesse oblige*—how are they justifying it? Are they showing disciplined and experienced minds, are they capable of maintaining a mature and informed disinterestedness, a humane and elevated serenity, in all their views of human life? Do they display invariably the imperial distinction of spirit, the patrician fineness of taste, which we have been taught to associate with that degree of proficiency in the liberal arts? We cannot see that the kind of discipline to which you say they have been subjected, has any such bearing. Gymnastics, copy-editing, stenography, food-etiquette, home laundering, and such like, are commendable pursuits, and we are all for having them well and freely taught, but we cannot see that they tend in the least towards what we have always understood an advanced degree in the liberal arts to mean. Therefore if you ask us to congratulate you on the number of your graduates, we must first have a look at their quality."

But if our system is doing as well as all this, you may say, if it turns out to be so much on the right track, after all, why trouble oneself about it, especially if the only changes one can suggest are a trifling matter of nomenclature and the suppression of a little forced play with formative knowledge? Well, I do not press either suggestion, even though I think that the matter of nomenclature is important because words have power. "The range of words is wide," says Homer; "words may tend this way or that way." A just care for words, a reasonable precision in nomenclature, is of great help in maintaining one's intellectual integrity. One can easily cheat oneself with words; one can as easily intoxicate oneself with them. But we may let this go; I should not be over-critical of our system on these grounds; I should not be disposed, in fact, to bear very heavily on its defects when reckoned against its excellences, were it not for just one matter to which we have not yet directed our attention.

XI

THIS matter is the status of the educable person. Hitherto our observations have been only upon the status of the ineducable in our régime; we have said nothing about the educable. Such persons exist among us, and in about as considerable numbers, I should say, as exist elsewhere. With reference to them we may observe, first, that they are socially valuable, they are a potential asset; and second, that our system does not, and by the conditions of its theory cannot, do anything whereby we may realise on their value. They simply go to waste, and as matters stand, they must do so. This consideration is the only thing that has seemed to myself to justify me in occupying your attention with this subject; the only thing, in fact, that makes the subject interesting to me. Our system, our new type of institutional organisation and influence, does everything, probably, that can be done for the ineducable, for the motor-minded, for all types among those we have been considering. All honour to it for that! Clearly, then, if everybody were motor-minded, ineducable, without hope of development beyond adolescence, it would be an excellent system indeed. If, again, the educable individual were socially valueless, one would be sorry for his misfortunes, of course, but one would hardly feel it worth one's while to parade them before this assemblage, nor could one hope to arouse more than an eleemosynary interest in them. But if the educable person be admitted to exist among us and to be worth developing; and if it be shown that our system not only does not, but under its theory cannot, direct and promote his due development, then, I think, the time that we have devoted to the examination of this theory has not been spent in vain.

We need not waste words over the assumption that the educable person exists here. We have always had him with us, so it would be fair to suppose *a priori* that his breed has not completely died out. Besides, we occasionally see him; not often, but often enough to suggest that he does not exist as a mere survival, a *dodo solitarius*, but that he is produced about as regularly as ever. We need not, I repeat, occupy ourselves with his vital statistics. We may, however, briefly examine one or two of our main reasons for thinking that the educable person is, from a social point of view, worth consideration, and that in behalf of the common welfare, something should be made of him.

The educable person, in contrast to the ineducable, is one who gives promise of some day being able to think; and the object of educating him, of subjecting him to the Great Tradition's discipline, is to put him in the way of right thinking, clear thinking, mature and profound thinking. Now, the experienced mind is aware that all the progress in actual civilisation that society has ever made has been brought about, not by machinery, not by political programmes, platforms, parties, not even by revolutions, but by right thinking. One feature appears with unfailing regularity upon the long panorama of human activity which our discipline exhibits to us. We see there that every social enterprise, every movement, every policy, which was not conceived in right thinking and carried out under the direction of right thinking, has in the long-run cost more than it came to. Nature, if you like that term, has levied a fine on it, proportioned with interesting precision to the degree of its departure from the counsels of right thinking. Our discipline enforces no more weighty and memorable lesson than this. Nature takes her own time, sometimes a long time, about exacting her penalty, and often gets at it by strange, unexpected and roundabout ways; but exact it in the end she always does, and to the last penny. It would appear, then, that a society which takes no account of the educable person, makes no place for him, does nothing with him, is taking a considerable risk; so considerable that in the whole course of human experience, as far as our records go, no society ever yet has taken it without coming to great disaster. It has been tried before; as I said, the testimony of our discipline is most impressively explicit on this point. It has been tried before by societies relatively as rich, powerful, self-assertive and self-congratulatory as ours—the glib complacency of Mr. Hoover in his public utterances is, one may say, word for word the glib complacency of Cleon or of Trajan in theirs—but none has ever yet succeeded in safely putting that risk at defiance.

At present our society is in most serious economic difficulties. The truly mature person, bred in the Great Tradition, could at any time have reached into his accumulation of experience and found a match for each one of these difficulties, and for every circumstance of each, every sequence of cause and effect. The happenings of the last eight or ten years have simply added another set of stereotyped registrations to his stock of experience. There is nothing new about them, nothing strange or unpredictable. Yet I am sure you have remarked, as I have, the extraordinary, the unconscionable incompetence with which these happenings have been met by those whom our society regards as its "leaders of thought." Indeed, the universality of this incompetence and its incredible degradation are perhaps all that puts a distinguishing mark on the circumstances of the period. I may give one example. One of the men most in the public eye holds a high place in industry and finance.

IN THE UNITED STATES

All his sayings and doings are made much of in the press, which represents him as a person of almost unearthly wisdom. His prominence in some international transactions a short time ago made his name a household word. I think, though I am not quite sure, that he holds an honorary degree from Columbia University. After the depression had been running for about a year, a friend of mine who knows him very well met him, and said, "I suppose you have learned a good deal in these twelve months; tell me what you have learned." "Yes, indeed," he replied. "We have learned that it won't do to reduce wages." Think of it! To have gone through a year of economic convulsions of catastrophic importance, and to have learned *that!* One might suppose that the survivor of a deluge, say some Hasisadra or Noah, or one who had lived through the subsidence of Atlantis, as Plato describes it, would see point to digging into the natural laws that govern such happenings and finding out all he could about them, in the hope of turning up something that might be useful in the event of their threatened recurrence. Suppose

THE THEORY OF EDUCATION

you met one of these survivors and asked what he had learned from his experience, and he told you with a great air of finality that he had learned that it is a good thing to go in when it rains! A most incompetent answer, you would say, a childish answer, the effort of an immature, ineducable mind. Yet not one whit more so than the answer given by this person, to whom the nation, in a sense, looks up.

You may easily see the bearing that all this has upon our subject. If you are not by this time tired of having me use my university as a *corpus vile* for anatomical purposes, I will venture to bring it forward once more. Last summer, in a speech at Paris, Mr. Butler spoke of Russian economic competition and the Five-Year Plan. He made the excellent and salutary observation that the Five-Year Plan, whether a good, bad or indifferent plan, was a plan, and that the rest of the world was planless. "I have great concern for the man with a competing social and economic system, if we do not demonstrate the supremacy of ours. I have great concern for the man with a plan, competing with a planless world." This is admirable; it touches the marrow of our good sense. "What I ask for," Mr. Butler continued, "is a plan; a plan to solve problems that have become international. Not to sit and wait, not to stand and wait, not to abuse the people with a plan, but to present a better plan. . . ."

Just so. It seems competent then, in the first instance, to say to Mr. Butler, "You ask for a plan—very well, produce one. Produce one that shall take strict and logical account of every economic factor in the situation. It can be done. But the plan must be one that shows *the same integrity of purpose in its construction that is apparent in the Five-Year Plan;* otherwise it will get nowhere. Do not speak of the League of Nations; we have seen leagues of nations before, all the way back to the Amphyctionic League; we know all about them, what their real purpose and function are, and we can recognise at a glance every specious pretext under which these have ever been disguised. Do not, moreover, give your plan a political character or attempt a political approach to the problems with which it proposes to deal. We know what political government is, its history, and the limitations under which it must work, the limitations put upon it by its primary intention and character, and there is no use trying to make anything in the realm of politics and statecraft stand up to the Five-Year Plan; the first collision will break it into kindling-wood."

So we might say; and Mr. Butler could produce such a plan with no great effort and no very heavy investment of originality. But producing a plan is not everything; one must also get it accepted, and the first thing needful towards getting it generally accepted is its acceptance by a body, large or small, of informed and intelligent opinion. Now, suppose Mr. Butler produced his plan, could he find in this country, or could there be found for him, such a body of opinion to understand, accept and support it? Quite clearly no such body of opinion could be found. Those who most naturally would first take the plan under review are such as the gentleman I just now mentioned as having learned so much from the country's recent economic experiences—one could run off their names from memory, hardly missing a single one—and you can imagine what that order of intelligence would make of it. Your imagination will at once supply, without any aid from me, a sense of what the upshot of the plan would be, and this will be enough, and more than enough, to convince you that Mr. Butler's demand for a plan amounts to a counsel of perfection.

Well, then, that being so, it seems to me quite competent for us to turn on Mr. Butler, and ask what Columbia University has been about all these years. If it had retained the character of an educational institution, devoting itself to educating educable persons, making this its primary interest, it would now, probably, by itself alone, be contributing a pretty fair quota towards a body of opinion intelligent enough, at least, to know a sound plan when it saw one. Formerly, Columbia turned out a respectable number of such individuals. The educable person is still here in the raw, and a few of his kind, as a finished product, would come in uncommonly handy at the moment. What has Columbia to say in the premises? What has our whole educational system to say?

The question is pertinent. The sum of the matter is that when circumstances tighten up, and profound, disinterested thought is called for, it becomes manifest that the newer type of institutional organisation and influence does not fill the bill. One may say generally that in its utter helplessness with the educable person it does not fill the bill in any circumstances. We citizens of the republic of letters have no wish to escape the responsibility of saying just this, and we do say it. But in particular we remark also that at times like the present the anti-social character of this type of organisation is most clearly apparent. Our society can get along for considerable periods by the process known as "muddling through," in more or less cheerful disregard of the absence of thought and intelligence. We take up the tabernacle of Moloch and Chiun, our images—Mr. Coolidge's two-gallon hat and Mr. Henry Ford's conveyor-system—and follow the star of our god Buncombe along ways which seem not too insecure. But occasionally circumstances arise which make it imperative that some one should do some thinking, even as Mr. Butler suggests; and in its utter incompetence with the only person among us who gives promise of ever being able to think, our newer type of institutional organisation has failed us so notably that the term *anti-social*, applied to its character, seems neither unjust nor inurbane.

XII

NEVERTHELESS we must be careful to observe that this slighting of the educable person has not been deliberate, wilful or heedless; nor has it ever failed to give rise to great searchings of heart, even among those who are obliged to fall in with it. My impression is, as I have already said—and I give it wholly under correction and for what it is worth—my impression is that a great deal of the general dissatisfaction with our system may be run directly back to this root. I suspect, though I say it with all delicacy and diffidence, that this is largely the ground of Mr. Butler's discontent, and that the ground of his anxiety is the apparent assurance that, as things stand, nothing in the world can be done about it. Of course, working under the prescription of an impossible theory is attended by a continual sense of frustration, impotence and failure—this is always bound to be the case, it must be so—but I believe that this sense is most acutely felt at this point. I have heard say

THE THEORY OF EDUCATION

that professional teachers tend to become petty and ingrowing. I do not know that this is so, but if it be so, there is surely some extenuation to be found in the theoretical conditions under which they exercise their calling.

Mr. Flexner says that "a student of Columbia College may study serious subjects in a serious fashion." I do not know just what he means by this. On the face of it, the statement is commonplace; anybody anywhere may study serious subjects in a serious fashion. The things to be considered, assuming that he be educable as well as serious, are what he gets out of it, and whether his circumstances permit him to get enough out of it to make his exertions worth while. If Mr. Flexner means that an educable person can in any proper sense of the term get an education in Columbia College, I must disagree with him. I firmly believe that no such thing is possible; and now, with your permission, I will skirt the margin of good taste by saying that I firmly believe no such thing is possible in any American institution with which I am acquainted.

Why should this be so? Let me put it this way: Why is it impossible for Columbia to be a training-school for the ineducable with one side of its being, and an educational institution for the educable with the other? I cannot answer that question. There seems no reason for it *a priori*. Would not a mere slight mechanical rearrangement easily bring the thing about—so-much institutional energy and attention sluiced off to turn the one set of wheels, so-much sluiced off to turn the other? It would seem so. There is certainly no indisposition on the part of the authorities towards anything of the kind; quite the contrary. There is no prejudice or prepossession against the educable person; all hands are ready to do their best by him, they are more than willing, they would gladly make every effort compatible with the general theory that governs their procedure. So much is true also, probably, of the average run of our institutions; we may at any rate well believe it is true of them. But there seems to be somewhere in the order of nature some obscure and powerful factor making steadily against any sort of success worth speaking of.

When we talk about the order of nature, or a law of nature, we mean no more than a registration of experience. The final "causes of things," so wistfully apostrophised by Lucretius, seem forever beyond us, even the causes of the most commonplace phenomena. We are fond of thinking we have solved a problem of cause and effect, when all we have done, really, is to move it a step or two backward. We say that when bodies, free to fall, fall always down and never up, they do so in obedience to the law of gravitation; but we really know of no such law. What we mean is that in all human experience free bodies have invariably behaved in that way, and this gives rise to a correspondingly strong expectation that they will continue to behave in that way; but of any "law" compelling them to do so, we know nothing. Some years ago I was in Turin, where bakers were trying to make a certain breadstuff as it was made in Genoa, only a few miles away. They could not do it. They brought down flour from Genoa, they brought down workmen, they even brought down water in casks, they reproduced every condition of Genoese manufacture as far as human intelligence could discern them, but with no success. No one could account for this; probably no one ever will; so we say there was something in the order of nature against the project. One of our physicists, the other day, speaking of a magnet's pull on steel, said he could clear the problem, perhaps move it one or two steps backward, but as for solving it, the best he could do was to say that the magnet pulled on the steel because God willed it should do so. Consider the simplest and most obvious commonplaces of observation, the periodicity of hay fever, the phenomena of measles or seasickness, or even the distribution of hair on the human body —no one on earth knows or can surmise any more plausible final reason for them than that God wants them to be that way.

Thus I cannot answer our question why our institutions may not deal satisfactorily with the ineducable and the educable at the same time. We only know that with every exercise of good will in the premises, they do not, apparently cannot, and for all we can see, never will; so we say that there seems to be something in the order of nature against their so doing, some principle to which the attempt at this procedure is repugnant. *They fought from heaven,* cried Deborah; *the stars in their courses fought against Sisera.* In the realm of the spirit, as of the flesh, certain salutary ways, certain lines of wholesome and rewarding procedure, seem to be marked out for us, and we cannot profitably transgress them. Such knowledge of them as we have is empirical and tentative. All we really know of them, indeed, is that they are there; and we remember the noble passage, grand with all the grandeur of a chorus of Æschylus, in which Bishop Butler insists that the imperfection of man's knowledge is all the greater reason for his strict obedience, as far as his knowledge goes, in order that "he may never make the dreadful experiment of leaving the course of life marked out for him by nature, whatever that nature be, and entering upon paths of his own, of which he can foresee neither the dangers nor the end."

But a recapitulation of some of the matters that we have already observed will go some way, perhaps, towards making this incompatibility of function seem reasonable. How is it possible, really, as a matter of what old-school psychologists called "the common sense of mankind," for an institution to affirm a pseudo-equalitarian, pseudo-democratic theory at one end of its campus, and deny it at the other? How can it effectively honour the Great Tradition on one side of the street, and disparage it on the opposite side? How can it effectively maintain a Holmes, Lowell, Adams, Pancoast, Humphreys, Osler, Gildersleeve, in one set of buildings while devoting another set to their practical extermination? One is reminded, though the parallel is possibly not quite exact, of the French painter's acute observation that art cannot be incorruptible part of the time. One is also reminded of the formula known in economics as Gresham's law, that "bad money drives out good"; the two cannot exist in circulation side by side, and it is always the good money that is forced out. I do not mean to imply that the work of the training-school is bad money; on the contrary, I have taken pains to express my great respect for it, my appreciation of the need of it, and my wish that it could be extended. I mean only that it is in all respects so different from the work of an educational institution that the attempt to compass both under the same general direction is bound to be ineffectual, and that the mere force of volume would always tend to drive the latter out.

XIII

WE SAID at the outset that this discussion could not be made to lead to any practical, or rather practicable, conclusion, and we are now at the point where we must face that embarrassment. Things being as they are, one's natural desire is to see what can be done about them. Frankly, I do not see that anything can be done about them. There is no trouble about seeing what might be done, perhaps what should be done, but what can be done is another matter. First let us see what we citizens of the republic of letters, mindful of Plato's injunction, think might be done. We would say to ourselves first, "The whole theory on which we are working is egregiously wrong, unsound, absurd, and there is no possible compromise with an unsound theory; nature always steps in and exacts her penalty. Ignorance is no excuse with her; good intentions are no extenuation. Our system does many good things, it has much more good in it than bad, but the good things it does

THE THEORY OF EDUCATION

are done under the sanction of an unsound theory, and incur the penalties that nature always lays on such enterprises. Therefore the only policy is one of 'thorough.' Let us simply discard this unsound theory, and substitute a sound one, one that answers to the facts of experience, just as we discarded Ptolemaic astronomy for Copernican, and as we substituted chemistry for alchemy. Pseudo-equalitarian and pseudo-democratic ideas have no place in educational theory, so let us make a clean sweep of them, and rearrange our practice accordingly."

This would indeed be no very exorbitant proposal, no more so than a proposal to abandon the geographical theory of Cosmas Indicopleustes or the cosmogony of the book of Genesis. Yet it could not be carried out; you may perceive at once that it could not be carried out, for very powerful collateral interests have grown up around our theory, tending to hold it firmly in place. Mention of the Mosaic cosmogony suggests a parallel; you are, of course, aware of the very strong institutional interest which we may almost say is built into that theory, and you know how long the strength of that interest has enabled the theory to hold out. You know the story of Galileo's collision with a similar institutional interest. Some great man of the last generation, I think Professor Huxley, though I am not quite sure, said bitterly that plenty of people would be found to deny the law of gravitation if a collateral interest of this kind were opposed to it. Just here, again for example, comes in the difficulty of discarding or even revising the extraordinary and remarkable official theory on which the United States is attempting to deal with the liquor traffic. Experience has made it clear beyond doubt or peradventure that prohibition in the United States is not a moral issue; it is not essentially, even, a political issue; it is a vested interest.

Our educational system is thus in a plight closely corresponding to that of our economic system. Many people are uneasy about our economic system; as you know, experience is forcibly directing attention to it, with the result that its unsoundness of theory is becoming more and more clearly apparent. Many people think it should be changed, even radically; there is no trouble about seeing just how it should be changed; but nobody is quite prepared to face the enormous deflation that would ensue if it were changed. One is reminded of the story of the boa-constrictor that swallowed a rabbit, then reached through a hole in a fence, and swallowed another. The bulk of the rabbits held the snake's body immovable in the hole; he could go neither forwards nor backwards. He could have backed out into freedom by disgorging the second rabbit, but he was not prepared to face this deflation; and so he died. Our economic system is in just that situation, and so, in all its essential respects, is our educational system. The general disposition would be to hold tight, like the snake, yielding nothing, and hoping vaguely that some saving intervention might come along to cut in between cause and effect. This disposition is no doubt profoundly unintelligent; the entertainment of this hope is quite unhistorical—no such hope was ever yet rewarded. But we all know that this disposition is what a sound and really effective reform of our system would chiefly have to reckon with.

Here, however, I should like to enter a caveat against possible misunderstanding. My observation of human nature is by no means so superficial as that I should for one moment intimate this disposition to be wholly that of Alexander the coppersmith, arising from individual fear of being put out of business. The revision of our educational theory would of itself put no one out of business; on the contrary, we would all have more business, better business, and be able much more to enjoy our devotion to it. The narrowest trade-unionist view of the situation could discern nothing to be afraid of; better far all round, I should say, if there were everything for it to be afraid of. No, what I have in mind as determining this disposition is chiefly the composite force of inertia, diffidence, preoccupation, a kind of timidity that looks on *omne ignotum pro magnifico,* infirmity of purpose, the tendency to absorption in one's immediate interests and surroundings, deference to convention, and so on; all which may be put down as

IN THE UNITED STATES

among the weaknesses of our common humanity, and not to be judged on moral grounds too harshly, if at all. Side by side with these goes one very curious and interesting trait, perhaps the most illogical to be found in all human nature's apparently limitless resources of bad logic; and upon this, on account of its particular interest, I shall dwell for a moment.

I refer to the strange inexplicable loyalty that the average person seems to feel called upon to exercise towards a system out of which he has in one way or another done well, or perhaps only passably well, even though in his heart he disbelieves in it, disapproves of it, and would gladly sacrifice the prospect of any further actual gain for the satisfaction of seeing it abolished. This, too, is not a trait that we need feel called upon to judge. All we need do is to examine it, remark its strangeness, and take account of its bearing on our subject. Let me recount one or two instances where it has fallen under my own observation in what seemed to me a notable way. Four or five years ago I was passing through the lobby of a hotel in New York, in company with an acquaintance who had been one of the world's foremost financiers, but was then retired. There was a broker's office in the hotel, and we stopped for a moment to look at the quotations. After we had watched them awhile, my friend said to me in an undertone, "This is a filthy business; we are merely gambling in the sweat of a lot of poor men." He was very rich; he did not care if he never turned another penny in his life. Moreover, he no longer had any associations or commitments to consider, and no friends who would have thought a whit the less of him for the public expression of his honest opinion on any subject. He also knew the economics of stock-market transactions like a book, knew just what he was talking about, and could give chapter and verse for it to any one who might undertake to discuss their ethics with him. Yet he would never say publicly what he said behind his hand to me; it would be impossible to get him to do it. I urged him to come out with it; business was then running up to the present crisis, and I thought the public expression of his views would do some good, as I still think it might, very probably would, have done. But he never spoke out; and for no conceivable reason except the inhibitions put upon him by this curious, illogical—as far as I can see, indefensible—sense of loyalty to an economic system which he knew was thoroughly bad, for which he felt a corresponding contempt and disgust, but out of which he had done well.

A second instance concerned another friend in the business world, one of the ablest and best men I ever knew, and one of the most successful. You cannot identify him by anything I say, or even identify the part of the world he lives in, so I am risking no breach of promise in speaking of him. I saw him about a month after the great collapse of the stock-market two years ago, and he treated me to a half-hour of the most searching and salty analysis of the situation. In the course of it, to illustrate a point he was making, he told me he had some little holding or other lying around in Wall Street that he had forgotten all about, and could have manipulated a profit of $150,000 on it.

"But I didn't take that profit," he said, beating his desk with his fist, "and I didn't take it *because —I—didn't—want it*. I didn't *need* it; and I knew it would come out of elevator-boys, clerks, manicures, stenographers and all sorts of people who couldn't afford to lose. I don't like that kind of money." Then at once he said, "Now, don't you ever tell a soul in the world that I have been talking to you in this way." He was so concerned, you see, lest some one should know he had not played the game by the rules, not taken his profit, not let conventional ethics stand above humanitarian considerations; he was so fearful of the implied criticism on an economic system which he regarded as despicable but out of which he had done well, that he repeatedly insisted I should never betray him.

So it seems that dissatisfaction with our system, however acute and widespread, is unlikely to take shape in flat abandonment of our educational theory; and short of that, it would appear that nothing can be done which would go any great way towards mending matters, nothing that would bring out the educable person and set him right with the world. The educational system of Continental countries, like Mr. Jefferson's, tends primarily towards salvaging the educable person, seining him out of the general ruck, and making something of him. It does this easily, naturally, purposefully, because it is not hamstrung by any insane pseudo-equalitarian and pseudo-democratic notions about education; it imports into its practice no such irrelevant nonsense as those notions entail. It is based on the idea that educable persons are relatively few, that their social value is great, that they are accordingly precious and should be enabled to make the most of themselves. It does reasonably well by the ineducable also, but it has no sentimental or romanticist view of his capacities; it gives him such training as he is able to accept, unornamented by finical stuff corresponding to that with which our theory obliges us to decorate our training, such, for example, as our "courses in English," "reading periods," and the like. My impression is that the proportion of naturally ineducable persons runs about as high in European populations as in ours. European systems, however, do not go through the specious and immoral pretence of educating them; they do not pretend that when they are through processing a proverbially refractory raw material, the product is a silk purse or anything in the least like a silk purse. They are realistic, they see things as they are; and they stand in this sharp contrast to our system because their theory is sound, while ours is unsound.

Private enterprise in this country, it is true, might establish a set of institutions for the educable only, consecrated to an unswerving service of the Great Tradition; this would consist of a secondary school, an undergraduate college, and a university comprising the four traditional faculties of Literature, Law, Theology and Medicine. But for obvious reasons this set of institutions would stand a long time with its doors locked, waiting for eligible persons to seek it out. Then when it began to exist as a going concern, it would be existing against all the force of wind and tide, under every temptation to eviscerate itself by concession and compromise. If it kept to its intention, it would of course triumph gloriously in the long-run; but the run would be so long, and the chances of its fidelity so doubtful, that private enterprise, however enlightened and public-spirited, could hardly be expected not to hesitate. Then, too, there is the question of the administration of this wholly alien enterprise. Where the Great Tradition is concerned, "plant" is secondary; throughout the long course of its history, as we have seen, the individual and his groupings have been the primary thing. I am reminded of the profound and delicate words of the *Imitation*, that superbly profound and delicate work of an author who chose to remain unknown, content that his name should be written only in the Book of Life. "It is *a great art*," says the author of the *Imitation*, "to know how to converse with Jesus." Truly it is; it is an art of which a lifetime's learning gives but the most beggarly rudiments. Even so may we say that it is a great art to know how to be on living terms with the Great Tradition. We who call ourselves continuators of the Great Tradition are aware with bitterness that in so styling ourselves we are but voicing an aspiration, we are but offering our reverence to a distant, high and unapproachable ideal. We know better than any one can tell us, how slight is our proficiency in the great art of familiar converse with it. Well, then, in a society that not only has lost that art but has lost even the knowledge that such an art exists, a society in which the Great Tradition itself is in complete abeyance—but I think I need say no more, the conclusion is manifest, it is inescapable.

XIV

But, sterile as this conclusion may be, sterile as in a sense all our conclusions may be, they tend neither to despondency nor to feebleness of endeavour. I may remind you—though I should not say that; let me rather say I may put into words what I know is in the consciousness of us all—that the Great Tradition will be no man's debtor. When we speak of promoting it or continuing it, we are using a purely conventional mode of speech, as when we say that the sun rises or sets. We can do nothing for the Great Tradition; our fidelity to it can do everything for us. Creatures of a day, how shall we think that what we do or leave undone is of consequence to that which abides forever? Our devotion, our integrity of purpose, our strictness of conscience, are not exercised in behalf of the Great Tradition, but in our own behalf. Our recreancy cannot weaken it, our faithfulness cannot strengthen it; we alone are damaged by the one and edified by the other. The

Great Tradition is independent of us, not we of it. We can not augment or diminish the force of its august and salutary laws; we can but keep to them, and therein find our exceeding great reward.

We have therefore no responsibility but the happy one of keeping our eye single to our own obedience. We need take no thought for the Great Tradition's welfare, but only for our own; it asks no protection or championship from us, and any volunteer service of this kind is mere officiousness. We need not enter into the anxiety of the prophet who reported to Jehovah that things were in the very worst way possible, the cult of Baal triumphant, the true believers dispersed, their priests and prophets slain with the sword, "and I, even I only, am left, and they seek my life to take it away." One is almost certain that behind this despairing speech lay the thought, "—and what *would* happen to the True Faith if they should catch me too?" You remember with what delicate and indulgent humour Jehovah took means to show him that the True Faith had resources of its own, that it could pretty well manage to worry along, and that he had better stop fretting about it, take a rest and get his nerves together, and then go on attending to his proper business.

We are called to be disciples, not energumens. The Great Tradition will go on because the forces of nature are on its side; it has on its side an invincible ally, the self-preserving instinct of humanity. Men may forsake it, but they will come back to it because they must; their collective existence cannot permanently go on without it. Whole societies may disallow it and set it at nought, as ours has done; they may try to live by ways of their own, by bread alone, by bread and buncombe, by riches and power, by economic exploitation, by intensive industrialism, quantity-production, by what you please; but in the end they will find, as so many societies have already found, that they must return and seek the regenerative power of the Great Tradition, or lapse into decay and death.

I leave you, then, with this reassurance. Seeing things as they are, we perceive that the phase of life which appears peculiar to our own little point of time and our little section of human society, is in a very real sense no concern of ours; it is nothing to discourage or distress us, or to distract us from our duty of diligent and trustful obedience. It is only what, from the long-time point of view, we should expect. Two years ago I was in the museum at Bonn, where I saw the skull and other bony vestiges of the Neanderthal Man. He would seem to have been a terrible fellow in his day; and it is since his day, I presume, that most of the qualities which we regard as distinctively social have been developed in our race. Probably before and during his period the humanisation of man in society had not got very far. What impressed me most was that this period, distant as it may seem in the immediate view, is yet so recent that these frail fragments of a human or semi-human osseous structure still remain, that I can see and handle them; they have even retained their form so well that men of science are able to make a pretty plausible reconstruction of our departed brother's whole physique from the indications that they give. It is easy to run into a culpable cynicism in the expectations that we put upon humanity's

IN THE UNITED STATES

social development; yet the sight of our poor old relative's remains suggests very forcibly the ease with which those expectations may run into an equally culpable extravagance.

I do not think that our American society will ever return to the Great Tradition. I see no reason why it should not go on repeating the experience of other societies, having already gone as far as it has along the road of that experience, and find that when it at last realises the need of transforming itself, it has no longer the power to do so. The terrible words of Persius are as applicable to the tyranny of ideas as to any other mode of grasping and ruthless dictatorship. But this is no concern of ours. The Great Tradition has not left itself without abundant witness in contemporary societies, and as I began by saying, the constitution of the republic of letters knows no such thing as political nationalism. Our fellow-citizens are ours where we find them; and where they are not to be found we may regard ourselves as citizens *in partibus*, uncommitted to an officious and ineffectual evangelism. Our allegiance is to the constitution of our republic; we are committed only to clear understanding and right thinking. If our present discussion has been of any avail in encouraging these, we may perhaps believe that the intention of this Lectureship has been in some degree fulfilled.

Made in the USA
San Bernardino, CA
14 September 2017